THE ALPHABET BOOK

An ABC Book of Art, Rhymes, Patterns, and Activities

by Sharon Ralph

Incentive Publications, Inc.
Nashville, Tennessee

Illustrated by Dianna Meadows
Cover by Marta Drayton
Edited by Leslie Britt

ISBN 0-86530-307-X

Copyright ©1995 by Incentive Publications, Inc., Nashville, TN. All rights reserved. No part of this publication may be reproduced, stored in a retrieval system, or transmitted in any form or by any means (electronic, mechanical, photocopying, recording, or otherwise) without written permission from Incentive Publications, Inc., with the exception below.

Pages labeled with the statement ©1995 by Incentive Publications, Inc., Nashville, TN are intended for reproduction. Permission is hereby granted to the purchaser of one copy of THE ALPHABET BOOK to reproduce these pages in sufficient quantities for meeting the purchaser's own classroom needs.

PRINTED IN THE UNITED STATES OF AMERICA

Table of Contents

Preface vii

Suggestions For Use In The Classroom 9-11

Aa Is For Apple (Song) 12

Part One: Body Movements 13-20

Part Two: Materials And Directions For Alphabet-Art Activities 21-48

Part Three: Blackline Masters 49-78
    Picture Patterns 50-68
    Caption Rectangles 69-75
    Language Bubbles 76
    Cover Page For Student Books 77-78

Part Four: Extension Activities 79-83

Part Five: Pictures For Classroom Games 85-93

Literature Suggestions To Accompany Activities 94-96

Preface

The Alphabet Book is an exciting collection of activities designed for kindergarten, first, or second grade language arts programs. It is intended to foster problem solving, thinking skills, and creative thought and expression as children complete art activities for each letter of the alphabet.

After finishing the activities in this book, students will have completed a 26-page alphabet book which uses art activities as a learning tool to encourage independent reading and choral expression. These activities integrate each child's creativity into the learning process through the use of language bubbles (also known as "speech balloons," such as those used in comic strips). Music, movement, rhythm and rhyme, math skills, and creative writing, as well as alphabet, sound, and symbol practice provide a solid interdisciplinary approach to acquiring basic skills. The patterns provided for the art activities promote problem-solving strategies by supplying only part of the picture. It is left to the child to provide the needed missing parts. The art activities and body movements provide the children with ample opportunities to develop and practice hand-to-eye coordination as well as gross and fine motor skills.

A section of Extension Activities can be found at the back of the book. These enrichment activities extend opportunities for learning beyond the alphabet-art projects. Through dramatization and body movements, students practice letter recognition skills, handwriting skills, spelling, sight words, and much more.

The Alphabet Book is intended for the teacher who wants some new and exciting ideas and activities to enliven the language arts classroom. The activities in this book will have students singing, performing, problem solving, and learning all year long.

Suggestions For Use In The Classroom

Teacher-Made Classroom Book

It is recommended that you make a sample alphabet book to be used in the classroom. Since the student books will take some time to complete, a teacher-made classroom book will provide the students with practice in reading and serve as a visual aid as the children complete each letter's activity. You may want to have upper-level elementary students (in fifth and sixth grades) make the book for you. This will save you time, and these students will benefit from the bookmaking experience. Or, if you have the time, you may wish to make the classroom alphabet book into a "big book." A big book enables the entire class to see the print when reading it aloud. To do this, each blackline master pattern, as well as the text, should be enlarged. It is advisable to make the big book version out of tagboard or some other durable type of paper and to laminate the pages or cover them with contact paper.

Music And Movement

It is important that the children enjoy the singing of this book as well as practicing the body movements before attempting to learn the individual words of the text (see page 12 for the song "Aa Is for Apple" and pages 13-20 for the body movements). You may want to display the teacher-made classroom alphabet book for the entire class to see while the children sing the song and act out the movements for each letter. Turn each page in the book while the students are performing so that the illustrations serve as a visual clue or prompt. The students' familiarity to the words of the song and body movements is an important part of many of the extension activities (pages 79-83).

Student Books

The student books can be completed in a variety of ways, depending on your preference and the abilities of your students. For example, kindergarten teachers may wish to present one letter per week to their students. It does not matter whether the ABC sequence of letters is followed, since the student books will not be bound until all 26 activities have been completed. However, it is important that the students are familiar with the song "Aa Is For Apple," and have access to a teacher-made classroom book so that they may read and sing the book throughout the day. It is also a good idea to set up groups of students at "cutting and gluing" centers to complete the alphabet-art activities, with approximately four students working in each group.

First and second grade teachers may want to use these activities as a review at the beginning of the school year. These students can complete one alphabet-art activity per day with the entire class working at the same time on the alphabet page, or working at independent centers. When first and second grade students have completed all 26 activities, their alphabet books can help with additional class work. For instance, the teacher can ask such questions as, "Find and list all of the color words mentioned in your ABC book." "What words in the story rhyme with fed?" "What words throughout the story have the long o vowel sound?" etc. For more extension activities, see pages 79-83.

Blackline Masters

The blackline masters provide a stimulus for problem solving and creative thinking. Most of the patterns offer only part of the picture needed to complete the activity. It is up to the students to complete their own pictures for the books.

Language Bubbles

All children who make an alphabet book will have the opportunity to add their own creative thoughts and ideas to the activities, not only through their art work but also through the statements they create in the language bubbles. It is left to the teacher to decide how to best introduce the language bubbles in the classroom. You may choose to use the dictation process, in which you print into the language bubble exactly what a student has said. Another option is to have the child write his or her statement on a stick-on note or a piece of paper. This option gives the student a chance to experiment with his or her knowledge of print, using invented spelling to write the statement. Later you can read the statement and print it into the language bubble. Some students (second grade students, for example) may be able to write their statements in the language bubbles themselves.

Organizing Student Books

It is recommended that you make a file in which each child may store his or her completed alphabet-art activities. Even kindergartners can file their own papers (although perhaps not neatly). The files do need to be accessible to the students. It may be helpful to separate the class into groups (by sex, for example), and have the girls' folders in one open box and the boys' folders in another. This method makes for fewer files per box so that it easier for each child to find his or her file. It is also helpful for the file folders to be in assorted colors to aid in identification. When the children have several completed alphabet-art activities in their file, it is an excellent assignment to have them put their papers in alphabetical order. Extra copies of the patterns should always be available for students who are absent when particular activities are completed. It is also helpful to display an alphabet chart on the front of each file so that the child, or you, may mark off the letters that have been completed. It can be frustrating to bind the students' books only to discover that several students have not completed all of the activities. The alphabet chart helps to keep track of who has completed what.

Aa	Bb	Cc	Dd	Ee	Ff	Gg
Hh	Ii	Jj	Kk	Ll	Mm	Nn
Oo	Pp	Qq	Rr	Ss	Tt	Uu
Vv	Ww	Xx	Yy	Zz		

The Child Who Enters School Mid-Year

For the teacher who makes the alphabet book a year-long project, there is always the question of what to do with the child who enters school mid-year. Two suggestions are offered. Designate some students to act as helpers to the new student. Divide the number of activities to be completed among the group. When each helper completes a page, have him or her write on the back, "To _____, From _____. Welcome to our class. Happy reading!" You may also let the new child take home an activity each night to be completed as homework. Whatever you decide, it is important to always have extra ready-to-use patterns on hand.

Binding Student Books

There are several options for binding the student books. In most cases, the books will be too thick to staple with an ordinary classroom stapler. The best method I have found is to bind the books on a binding machine using one-inch plastic binders. If you do not have access to one of these machines, another choice is to punch the pages with a three-hole punch and use metal rings to secure the book. (The two-inch round head paper fasteners, no. 7, will also work.) If you use paper fasteners, it is helpful to tape the back side of each book, so that the fasteners will not open and pull through. This also prevents the fasteners from catching on other things. Another choice is to punch the three holes on the side and tie the pages together with yarn. Finally, you can have each child purchase a plastic, three-ring notebook to serve as the cover of the book.

After The Books Are Bound . . .

. . . have a party! Your class can visit other classrooms and serenade them with their songs and activities. Children also love being able to share the books with their families. The students (and the teacher) are afforded with the sense of a job well done!

Ordering Materials To Make Student Books

Make a list of all of the materials you will need in order to complete the student alphabet-art books. To do this, look at the Materials List on the first page of each activity. You should also include on your list the materials needed to make the cover page of the book (see page 77). Most of the materials can be ordered through your school system's material supply center. However, since these orders usually take a long time to receive, it is best to order all of the materials needed for the student books at one time.

Aa Is For Apple

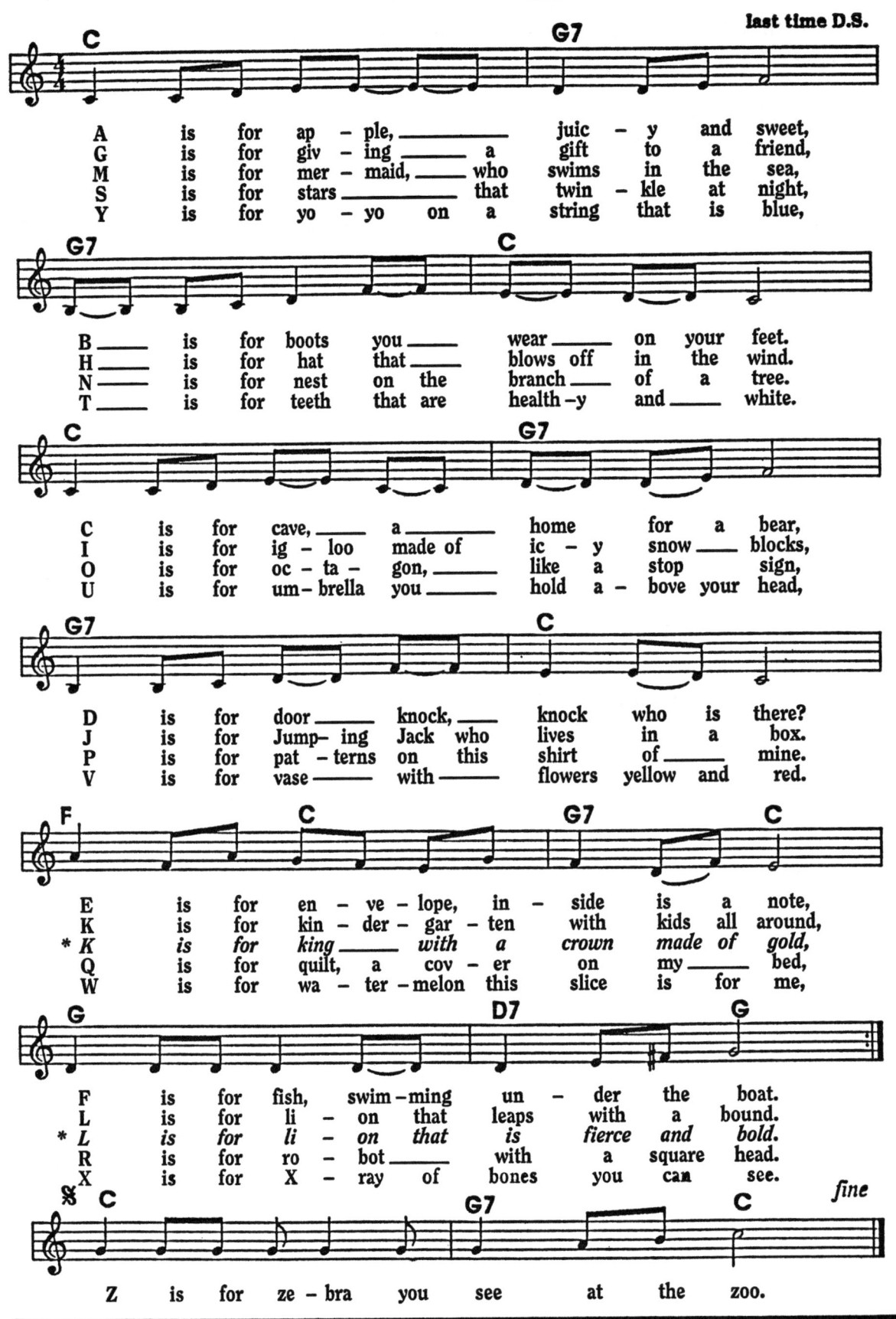

* Substitute these lines for use with first and second grades.

©1995 by Incentive Publications, Inc., Nashville, TN.

Part One

Body Movements

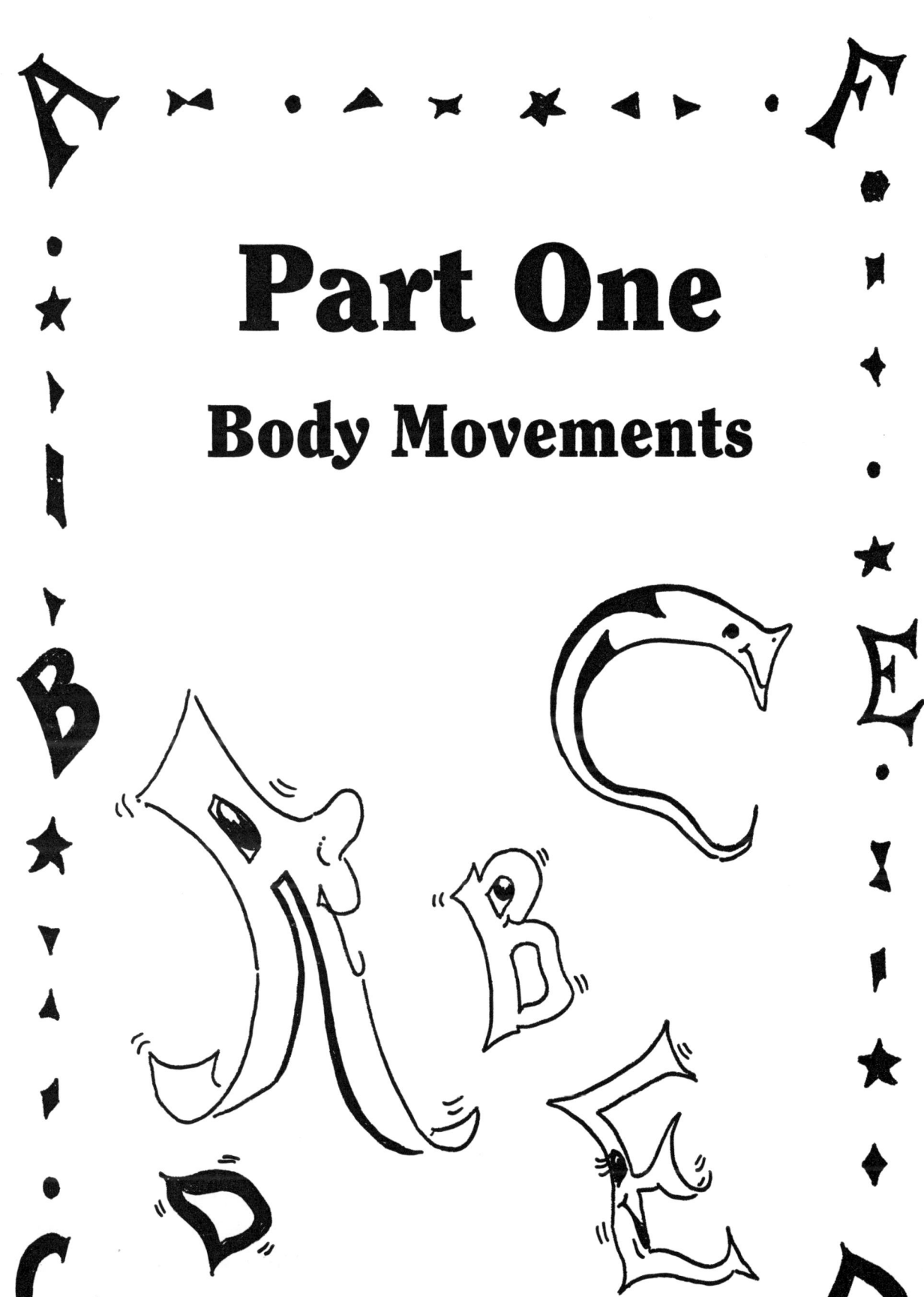

Aa is for apple,

Position your right hand in front of your chest and act as if you're holding an apple. Then pretend to take a bite of the apple.

juicy and sweet.

Rub your stomach in a circular motion.

Bb is for boots

With both index fingers, point to your feet.

you wear on your feet.

March in place.

Cc is for cave,

Holding both arms above your head, make a circle with your arms.

a home for a bear.

With arms bent in front of your chest, palms out, make the fingers of both hands look like the claws of a bear.

Dd is for door.

Using both index fingers, trace in the air the shape of a door, starting at the top.

Knock, knock, who's there?

With your right fist, pretend to knock on the door. Now, shrug your shoulders with palms flat and turned upward, making the body gesture to say, "I don't know!"

Ee is for envelope.

Pretend to hold both ends of an envelope in front of you.

Inside is a note.

Your left hand should pretend to hold the envelope, while your right hand pretends to pull the note out of the envelope. To do this, extend your right hand up and away from your left hand.

Ff is for fish,

Place both palms together in front of your chest. Your thumbs should be facing up, representing the fin of a fish. Keeping palms together, extend hands forward and away from the chest, moving them with a curving motion.

swimming under the boat.

Keeping your palms together, "dive" your hands in a downward motion as if to go under something.

Gg is for giving a gift

With hands in front of your chest, pretend to hold a big box.

to a friend.

Turn to a child standing next to you and pretend to give him or her the box by extending both of your your arms at the same time.

Hh is for hat

Place the palm of one hand flat on the top of your head, representing a hat on your head.

that blows off in the wind.

Extend your arm outward, as if the hat has just blown off your head.

Ii is for igloo

Holding both arms above your head, make a circle with your arms.

made of icy snow blocks.

Fold your arms in front of you and shiver.

Jj is for jumping jack

Squat to the floor, bend your arms, and hold your elbows next to your body. Cup your hands and act like you are peeking over the edge of a box.

who lives in a box.

Jump up from the squatting position.

Kk is for kindergarten
(for kindergarten classes)

Starting with your hands in front of your chest, extend your arms outward in a sweeping, open gesture, as if presenting the classroom.

with kids all around.

Using the index finger of your hand, point to various children in the class.

Kk is for king
(for first and second grades)

Stand straight and look quite proper, with your chin high in the air.

with a crown made of gold.

With both hands, pretend to hold a crown above your head.

Ll is for lion
(for kindergarten classes)

With fingers wiggling, hold your hands above your head and outline the shape of a lion's mane, making a circle above your head.

that leaps with a bound.

With both feet, take one jump forward. Make your fingers look like claws, and bare your teeth.

Ll is for lion
(for first and second grades)

Use the same body movements as above.

that is fierce and bold.

Make fingers look like claws. Bare your teeth.

Mm is for mermaid

Place your fingertips behind your neck with your elbows extended horizontally. Look glamorous!

who swims in the sea.

Use your arms to make swimming motions. (Kindergartners need to swim back to the spots where they were before leaping forward.)

Nn is for nest

Holding your hands in front of your chest, pretend to hold a bird's nest.

on the branch of a tree.

Standing straight, stretch out your arms and pretend to be a tree. Your body is the trunk, and your arms are the branches.

Oo is for octagon, like a stop sign.

Using both index fingers, quickly trace in the air the shape of an octagon, starting at the top.

Hold up one hand with your fingers straight and palm facing out to make the signal for stop, just as a police officer would do while directing traffic.

Pp is for pattern on this shirt of mine.

With one index finger, trace lines across your chest as if you are wearing a striped tee-shirt.

Form a fist with both hands, thumbs up. Now point to yourself with your thumbs.

Qq is for quilt, a cover on my bed.

Using both hands, pretend to pull up the covers of your bed to your chin.

Placing your palms together, position your hands to the side of your head, resting them against your cheek. Tilt your head in the direction of your hands and close your eyes.

Rr is for robot with a square head.

Walk stiffly in place while swinging your arms.

With palms facing out and thumbs extended, frame your head.

Ss is for stars

With one index finger, quickly point to various spots on the ceiling, as if you're pointing to stars in the sky.

that twinkle at night.

Make a tight fist with both hands, then quickly extend fingers outward. Quickly open and close your fists several times. You may want to move your hands around in various positions in front of you to represent many stars twinkling.

Tt is for teeth

With both index fingers, point to your teeth and grin.

that are healthy and white.

Using one hand, pretend to brush teeth with upward and downward strokes.

Uu is for umbrella

Using both hands, pretend to open an umbrella with one hand holding the handle and the other pushing open the umbrella.

you hold above your head.

Bend one arm and hold it in front of your chest, elbow pointing sideways. You are now holding your umbrella. When you sing or say the word "above," look up.

Vv is for vase

Pretend to hold a vase in front of your chest.

with flowers yellow and red.

With one hand holding the vase, the other hand makes motions as if putting long-stem flowers into the vase, one at a time.

Ww is for watermelon.

With your arms held in front of you, make the shape of a large watermelon.

This slice is for me.

Using both hands, act as if you're holding a big slice of watermelon up to your mouth. When you sing or say the words "for me," point to yourself.

Xx is for x-ray

Bend your arms and crisscross them, forming an X.

of bones you can see.

The fingertips of your hand should touch your rib cage. Bend your neck and look down at your chest.

Yy is for yo-yo

Point the index finger of one hand straight out with the thumb pointing up and the remaining fingers folded in. Pretend to work a yo-yo by bringing your hand up and down.

on a string that is blue.

With one hand, act as if you're holding one end of a string, while the other hand takes the opposite end of the string and stretches it outward.

Zz is for zebra

Stretch your fingers apart and place your hands sideways on your face with your fingers touching. Peek through the space between two fingers. You now have stripes on your face.

you see at the zoo.

With thumb and fingers curled, form circles around both eyes. You now have binoculars to see the zebra up close, since this one is out in a field grazing and not in a cage.

Part Two

Materials And Directions For Alphabet-Art Activities

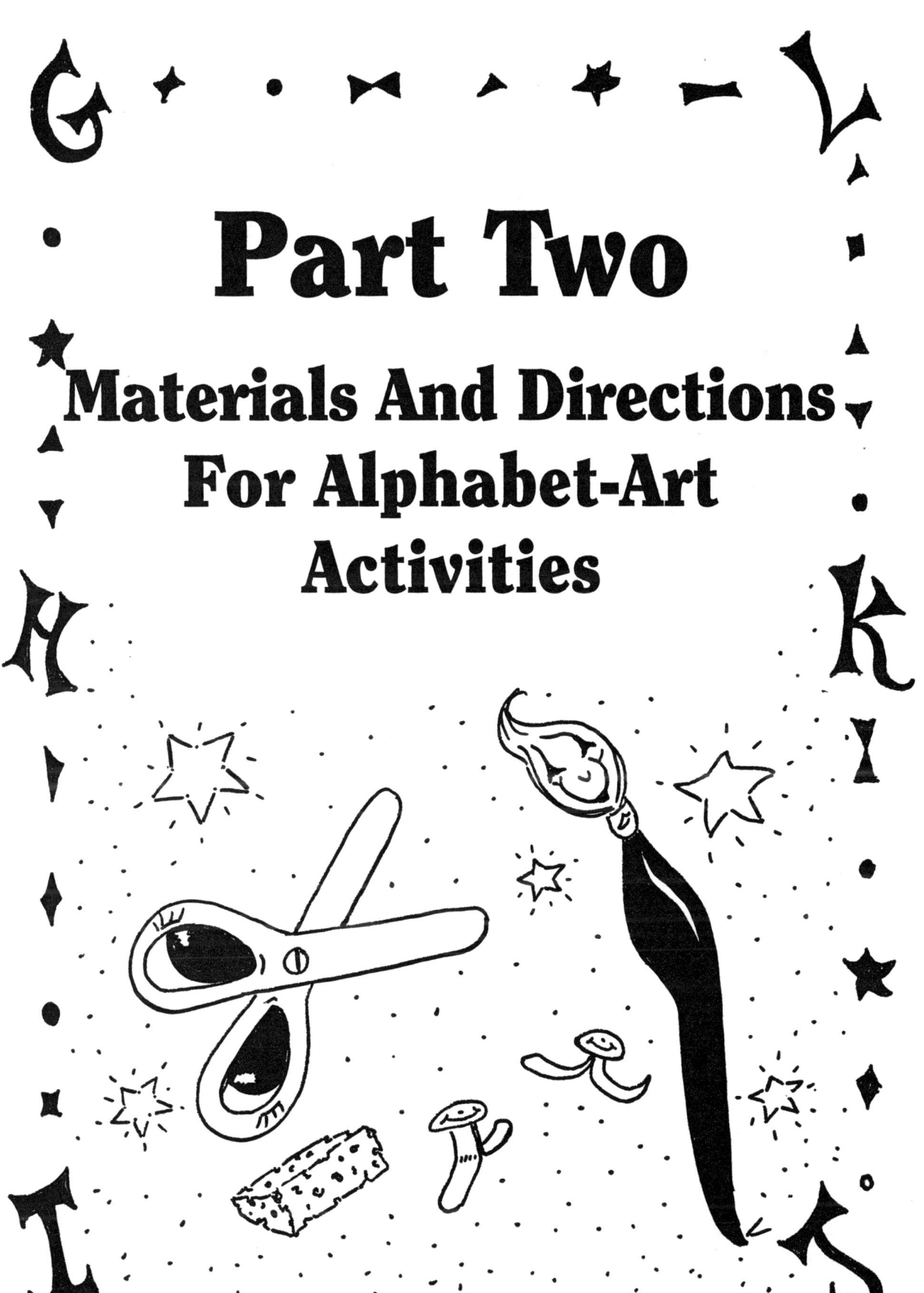

Aa Is For Apple, Juicy And Sweet

Materials

Each child will need:
- blackline master of apple, reproduced on white paper
- red, green, and brown construction paper, to be torn by students into small pieces
- 2" x 4" piece of yellow construction paper (for worm)
- 1½" x 1½" square piece of black construction paper (for hole)
- 9" x 12" royal blue construction paper for background page
- glue, glue stick, or paste
- scissors
- pencil and crayons
- caption rectangle reading "Aa is for apple, juicy and sweet."
- one language bubble

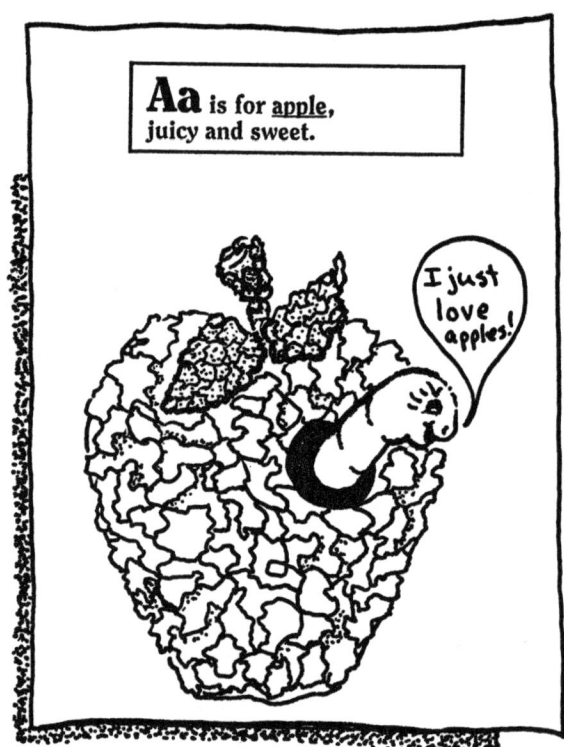

This activity involves making a mosaic apple from pieces of paper. The apple design will also include a black hole and a yellow worm.

Directions

1. Direct the students to cut out the caption rectangle reading "Aa is for apple . . ." and glue it to the top of the sheet of royal blue construction paper which will serve as the background page.
2. Students cut out the blackline master of the apple and glue it to the blue background page so that the bottom edge of the apple is near the bottom edge of the blue paper.
3. The students begin the apple mosaic by tearing small pieces of red paper and gluing the pieces to the white apple. Small pieces of green paper are used for the leaves, and small pieces of brown paper are used for the stem.
4. After the mosaic is completed, the students cut a circle out of the small square piece of black construction paper and glue the circle to the mosaic apple. (The black circle will represent a hole in the apple.)
5. The students then draw or color the front half of a worm on the 2" x 4" piece of yellow construction paper, cut it out, and glue it to the black circle on the apple. The worm should look as if it is coming out of the hole.
6. Finally, the students glue the language bubble in place. Direct the students to point the tip of the language bubble toward the mouth of the worm.

Bb Is For Boots You Wear On Your Feet

Materials

Each child will need:
- blackline master of boots, reproduced or traced on sturdy white stock paper
- manila or white construction paper, cut into a 6" x 10" rectangle
- 9" x 12" red construction paper for background page
- glue, glue stick, or paste
- scissors
- pencil and crayons
- caption rectangle reading "Bb is for boots you wear on your feet."
- one language bubble

Directions

1. Direct the students to cut out the blackline master of the boots and glue them to the bottom of the 6" x 10" sheet of manila or white construction paper. (The teacher of younger children may choose to have the boots cut out and ready for the children to glue into position.) Instruct the children that they have a choice concerning the position in which the boots are glued. The boots can be glued in a standing or walking position.

2. While the glue dries on the boots, the children can cut out the caption rectangle reading "Bb is for boots . . . " and glue it to the top of the red background page.

3. The students now draw or color a person wearing the boots. This requires a bit of thinking because the students should start with the legs and work up. The teacher may want to define and discuss the word "profile" with the students. Some children may want to draw a profile, or side view, of the person wearing boots if they chose to glue the boots in a walking position. (Profiles will be mentioned again in the Gg alphabet-art activity on page 28.)

4. After their person is complete, the students cut out the picture, leaving some white space around the person.

5. The picture is glued to the red background page.

6. Finally, the students glue the language bubble in place with the tip of the bubble pointing to the person's mouth.

Cc Is For Cave, A Home For A Bear

Materials

Each child will need:

- blackline master of cave, reproduced or traced on sturdy gray paper (construction paper or index stock paper will do; if you do not have gray paper, use white paper and have students color it gray)
- red, green, and brown construction paper, to be torn by students into small pieces
- 9" x 12" light blue construction paper for background page
- glue, glue stick, or paste
- scissors
- pencil and crayons
- caption rectangle reading "Cc is for cave, a home for a bear."
- one language bubble

Directions

1. Direct the students to cut out the caption rectangle reading "Cc is for cave . . ." and glue it to the top of the sheet of light blue construction paper which will serve as the background page.
2. Have students color the opening of the cave on the blackline master using a black crayon. Stress that they press hard on the crayon so that the opening is dark.
3. Have the students cut out the cave.
4. The students cut the opening of the cave on both sides, without cutting the top, so that the opening forms a flap.
5. Students glue the cave to the light blue background page, applying glue only on the outside edges of the cave. Stress the importance of not putting any glue on the opening flap. The opening must be free to lift.
6. Using crayons, the students color trees, bushes, etc., in the areas around the cave. Lifting the flap, the students either draw or color a bear inside the cave. They may wish to color the area around the bear darker, as it would look inside a cave.
7. Finally, the students glue the language bubble inside the cave with the tip pointed toward the bear. (Remind the students to use only a drop of glue on the language bubble so that the flap will not stick to the bubble.)

Dd Is For Door— Knock, Knock, Who's There?

Materials

Each child will need:
- blackline master of door, reproduced or traced on white construction paper or index stock
- 9" x 12" yellow construction paper for background page
- glue, glue stick, or paste
- scissors
- pencil and crayons
- caption rectangle reading "Dd is for door. Knock, knock, who's there?"
- two language bubbles

Directions

1. Direct the students to cut out the caption rectangle reading "Dd is for door . . ." and glue it to the top of the sheet of yellow construction paper which will serve as the background page.
2. Have students color the door and door frame on the blackline master.
3. Students cut out the door along the edges of the door frame.
4. Next the students carefully cut along the right side and top of the door so that it will fold open, away from the frame. The door frame should be glued to the yellow background page, leaving enough room on the right side of the page to draw or color a picture of a person. (Younger children may need help gluing their door to the page.) It is important not to get any glue behind the door. The door must be free to fold open.
5. The students draw or color a picture of a person standing by the door as if ready to open it. After doing this, students fold back the door and draw or color a picture of who, or what, is knocking on the door. (The children may draw anything from dinosaurs, monsters, and aliens to their friends or family members.)
6. Finally, the students glue a language bubble for the person answering the door and the person, or thing, behind the door. They might have to glue the language bubble on the back side of the door for lack of space anywhere else.

Ee Is For Envelope. Inside Is A Note

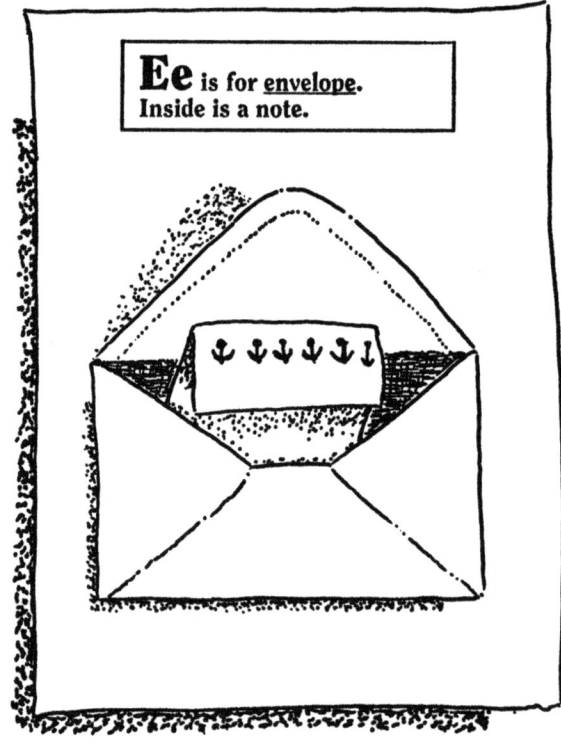

Materials

Each child will need:
- one 3⅝" x 6½" white envelope
- 8½" x 11" sheet of brightly colored paper
- 9" x 12" orange construction paper for background page
- glue, glue stick, or paste
- scissors
- pencil and crayons
- caption rectangle reading "Ee is for envelope. Inside is a note."

Directions

1. Direct the students to cut out and glue the rectangle reading "Ee is for envelope . . ." to the top of the orange background page.
2. Next students glue the front side of the white envelope to the orange background page, making sure that the flap easily opens and closes. Tell the students not to seal the envelope.
3. The students write a note on the 8½" x 11" colored sheet of paper. They can also decorate the page by coloring pictures on it.
4. When the note is finished, it is folded and placed inside the envelope.

Ff Is For Fish, Swimming Under The Boat

Materials

Each child will need:

- three or four blackline masters of the fish, reproduced or traced on orange construction paper
- one blackline master of the boat, reproduced or traced on brown construction paper
- 9" x 12" light blue construction paper for background page
- glue, glue stick, or paste
- scissors
- pencil and crayons
- blue tempera paint and brush to paint water scene, or one 5½" x 9" piece of royal blue construction paper to serve as water scene
- one wooden toothpick (optional)
- caption rectangle reading "Ff is for fish, swimming under the boat."
- two language bubbles

This activity includes a water scene in the picture. The teacher will need to decide whether to have the children paint the water scene, cut the water out of royal blue paper, or color the water scene with crayons.

Directions

1. If the water scene is to be painted, this needs to be done several hours in advance to allow time for the paint to dry. Direct the students to paint the lower half of the light blue background page so that the top of the water scene is a ripple or wave design. Cut out and glue the caption rectangle "Ff is for fish . . ." to the top part of the background page after the paint has dried.
2. If the water scene is to be cut from paper, direct the students to cut the top of the piece of royal blue construction paper into a ripple or wave effect so that it looks like water. They will then glue the royal blue paper to the light blue background page, making sure that the bottom corners of both papers match. Next have the students cut out and glue the caption "Ff is for fish . . ." to the top of the background page.
3. If the students are to color the water scene with crayons, have them do so and then attach the caption rectangle to the top of the background page.
4. The students cut out the brown boat from the blackline master and glue it to the background page. It should look as if it is floating on the water. Using a pencil or crayons, the students draw a person sitting (or standing) inside the boat. A wooden toothpick can represent a fishing pole, or the students can draw the pole themselves. If a toothpick is used, it will need to be glued to the page in an appropriate place.
5. The students cut the fish from the blackline masters and glue them below the boat.
6. Finally, students add to the picture the two language bubbles, one for the person in the boat and one for a fish.

Gg Is For Giving A Gift To A Friend

Materials

Each child will need:
- a square piece of wrapping paper (see blackline master for pattern)
- one 10" strip of bright colored yarn
- 9" x 12" yellow construction paper for background page
- glue, glue stick, or paste
- scissors
- pencil and crayons
- caption rectangle reading "Gg is for giving a gift to a friend."
- two language bubbles

The teacher may wish to define and discuss the word "profile" with the students. They will have the opportunity to draw or color the profiles of two people in this activity.

Directions

1. Direct the students to cut out and glue the caption rectangle to the top of the background page.
2. Next have them glue the square piece of wrapping paper to the center of the page.
3. The students now draw or color a person standing on each side of the piece of wrapping paper. The idea to be presented is one person giving a gift to another person.
4. The students tie the 10" piece of yarn into a bow and glue it on top of the wrapping paper. (Younger children will need help tying the bow.)
5. Language bubbles need to be glued for each person drawn.

Hh Is For Hat That Blows Off In The Wind

Materials

Each child will need:
- blackline master of the hat, reproduced or traced on brown construction paper
- one blackline master of the wind, reproduced or traced on light blue construction paper (this should be the same color as the background page)
- 9" x 12" light blue construction paper for background page
- glue, glue stick, or paste
- scissors
- pencil and crayons
- caption rectangle reading "Hh is for hat that blows off in the wind."
- one language bubble

Directions

1. Direct the students to cut out the caption rectangle "Hh is for hat . . ." and glue it to the top of the light blue background page.
2. Next, students cut out the wind circle from the blackline master and glue it on the top right-hand side of the background page, below the caption rectangle.
3. The brown hat is colored, cut out, and glued to the top left-hand side of the page, below the caption rectangle and across from the wind circle.
4. The students draw or color a face looking surprised or startled. It should be placed below the hat and wind. (The teacher may want to discuss with the children how someone's face looks when startled or surprised. It would be helpful to have the children act out an event that would startle or surprise someone and demonstrate how a surprised face might look.)
5. To complete the activity, a language bubble is placed near the face.

Ii Is For Igloo Made Of Icy Snow Blocks

Materials
Each child will need:
- one blackline master of the igloo puzzle pieces, reproduced or traced on sturdy white paper (construction paper or index paper)
- one blackline master of the igloo silhouette, reproduced or traced on white construction paper (optional)
- white tempera paint and brush
- cotton swabs
- adhesive spray and clear glitter (optional)
- 9" x 12" light blue construction paper for background page
- glue, glue stick, or paste
- scissors
- pencil and crayons
- caption rectangle reading "Ii is for igloo made of icy snow blocks."
- one language bubble

Directions
1. Direct the students to paint the bottom area (approximately 3" from the bottom edge) of the light blue background page with white tempera paint. Then have them print white spots above the painted area using a cotton swab dipped in the white paint to represent snowflakes in the sky. Allow time for the paint to dry before beginning the next step.
2. Students cut out and glue the caption rectangle "Ii is for igloo . . ." to the top part of the background page after the paint has dried.
3. Then the students cut out the blackline master of the igloo silhouette and glue it to the background page so that it rests upon the painted snow. (Older children may not need to have the shape of an igloo to help them put the puzzle pieces together. The teacher may wish to skip this step.)
4. The students cut apart the igloo puzzle pieces and arrange them into the shape of an igloo. The igloo silhouette will help the younger students arrange the pieces correctly. After the pieces have been cut out, they are glued to the white silhouette.
5. At this point the students draw or color a person standing in front of the igloo (in the area that is painted white).
6. A language bubble is then glued in an appropriate spot.
7. (Optional) To give the picture more of a wintry effect, the teacher may wish to spray the pictures with an adhesive spray and let the children sprinkle clear glitter onto the picture. Allow time to dry before filing.

Jj Is For Jumping Jack Who Lives In A Box

Materials

Each child will need:

- blackline masters of the jumping jack and box, reproduced or traced on sturdy white paper (construction paper or index stock)
- one round-head paper fastener
- 9" x 12" purple construction paper for background page
- glue, glue stick, or paste
- scissors
- pencil and crayons
- caption rectangle reading "Jj is for jumping jack who lives in a box."
- one language bubble

Directions

1. Direct the students to color and cut out the box and lid of the jumping jack. The students glue the box so that the bottom edge is approximately ¼" above the bottom edge of the purple background paper. Glue should be applied only to the sides and bottom of the box to allow the jumping jack to be slipped inside.
2. The lid of the box is placed on the top of the box so that it is lined up correctly, then attached at the right-hand end by a round-head paper fastener. The lid is lifted up to leave room for the jumping jack.
3. The students now need to color and cut out the pieces of the jumping jack and glue them together. The hat needs to be glued to the head before the facial features are added. Otherwise, the face of the jumping jack may be drawn too high on the face and some parts could be covered when the hat is added. The students may want to fold the body of the jumping jack accordion-style. This would give it the appearance of springing out of the box.
4. When the jumping jack is complete, it needs to be slipped into the box with its head and arms sticking out.
5. The students now cut out and glue the caption rectangle reading "Jj is for jumping jack . . ." to the top of the background page.
6. A language bubble can now be added in an appropriate spot.

Kk Is For Kindergarten With Kids All Around

(For Kindergarten Classes)

Materials

Each child will need:
- photocopies of student photos (school photos or teacher-taken photos can be arranged on one sheet of paper and photocopied)
- a photocopy of student signatures (see blackline master for name grid)
- 9" x 12" red construction paper for background page
- glue, glue stick, or paste
- scissors
- pencil
- caption rectangle reading "Kk is for kindergarten with kids all around."
- language bubble

Directions

1. Direct the students to cut out the caption rectangle reading "Kk is for kindergarten . . ." and glue it to the top of the red background page.
2. Next the students cut out the photocopied pictures of their classmates and glue them to the red background page. (It is a good idea to cut out one picture at a time and glue it to the page before cutting out another one. Children should also be encouraged to make rows of the pictures, leaving enough room beneath each picture for the signature.)
3. After all of the students' pictures have been glued to the background page, the students cut out and glue the photocopied signatures to the appropriate faces.
4. Each student then glues a language bubble by his or her face.

Kk Is For King With A Crown Made Of Gold

(For First And Second Grade Classes)

Materials

Each child will need:
- blackline master of the crown, reproduced or traced on sturdy yellow paper (construction paper or index stock paper)
- sequins, glitter, or small beads with which to decorate crown (optional)
- 8" x 8" sheet of white paper
- 9" x 12" red construction paper for background page
- glue, glue stick, or paste
- scissors
- pencil and crayons
- caption rectangle reading "Kk is for king with a crown made of gold."
- one language bubble

Directions

1. Direct the students to cut out the caption rectangle "Kk is for king . . ." and glue it to the red background page.
2. The students draw or color a picture of the face of a king on the 8" x 8" sheet of white paper. Encourage them to make the face as large as possible on the sheet. The king's face is cut out and glued to the red background page so that the chin of the king's face is near the bottom of the page.
3. The crown can then be colored, decorated, cut out, and glued to the top of the king's head.
4. Finally, a language bubble is glued near the king's mouth.

Ll Is For Lion That Leaps With A Bound
(For Kindergarten Classes)
Ll Is For Lion That Is Fierce And Bold
(For First And Second Grade Classes)

Materials

Each child will need:
- blackline master of lion, reproduced or traced on white or yellow construction paper or index stock
- orange tempera paint
- small sponge (approximately ½" x ½")
- clothespin (to hold the small piece of sponge)
- 9" x 12" light blue construction paper for background page
- glue, glue stick, or paste
- scissors
- pencil and crayons
- caption rectangle reading "Ll is for lion that leaps with a bound" for kindergarten students or caption rectangle reading "Ll is for lion that is fierce and bold" for first and second grade students
- one language bubble

The lion will have to be cut out and glued onto the light blue background page. If the teacher thinks the shape of the lion is too complicated for his or her students to cut out, below are listed some options for copying the lion.

- Trace and cut out the pattern of the lion onto a piece of cardboard. Have the children trace the lion directly onto the light blue background page and then color it yellow (the pattern of the lion will have to be traced onto the background page to look as if it is leaping or jumping, with front feet higher than back feet).
- Reproduce the blackline master of the lion directly onto the light blue background page, then have the children color the lion yellow.

Directions

1. Have the students cut out the appropriate caption rectangle and glue it to the top of the light blue background page.
2. Next, the students color yellow the blackline master of the lion, draw or color a face on the lion, and cut out and glue the lion to the background page, making sure that it is glued in a leaping position (front legs positioned higher than back legs). The students may want to add grass or bushes to the ground area of the picture.
3. Each student then sponge-paints the mane and tail of his or her lion. (Place the small piece of sponge between the clasps of a clothespin so that the sponge is held tightly. The student holds the opposite end of the clothespin and dips the sponge end into a small container of orange tempera paint.)
4. After the paint has dried, a language bubble is glued near the lion's mouth.

Mm Is For Mermaid Who Swims In The Sea

Materials

Each child will need:
- blackline master of mermaid tail, reproduced or traced on orange construction paper
- 9" x 12" light blue construction paper for background page
- glue, glue stick, or paste
- scissors
- pencil and crayons
- caption rectangle reading "Mm is for mermaid who swims in the sea."
- one language bubble

Directions

1. Direct the students to cut out the caption rectangle reading "Mm is for mermaid . . ." and glue it to the top of the light blue background page.
2. Then the students color (optional) the blackline master of the mermaid tail and cut it out. The tail is glued to the lower part of the background page, allowing room for the child to draw or color the upper body of the mermaid.
3. After the mermaid is complete, the students can color other items in the sea (fish, octopus, starfish, sea plants, sand on the ocean floor, etc.).
4. A language bubble can then be glued near the mermaid's mouth or near the mouth of a fish.

Nn Is For Nest On The Branch Of A Tree

Materials

Each child will need:
- blackline master of the nest, reproduced or traced on yellow construction paper
- 5" x 5" sheet of white paper
- brown and green tempera paint
- paintbrush
- sponge and clothespin for sponge painting
- 9" x 12" light blue construction paper for background page
- glue, glue stick, or paste
- scissors
- pencil and crayons
- caption rectangle reading "Nn is for nest on the branch of a tree."
- one language bubble

Directions

1. Each child will need to paint a branch on the lower half of a piece of light blue construction paper using brown tempera paint.
2. After the paint has dried, each child will sponge-paint green leaves on the branch using a small piece of sponge and a clothespin. (For detailed directions, refer to page 34.)
3. After all of the paint has dried, the students color the blackline master of the nest, cut it out, and glue it to an appropriate spot on the branch.
4. Next, the students draw or color eggs on the 5" x 5" piece of white paper, cut them out, and glue them inside the nest.
5. Students can now draw or color birds in the sky or on the branch. (The teacher may want to show the students how to draw birds using geometric shapes. See examples below.)
6. Clouds, a sun, and other outdoor items can be added. A language bubble is also placed on the picture in an appropriate place.

Oo Is For Octagon, Like A Stop Sign

Materials

Each child will need:

- blackline master of octagon, reproduced or traced on white construction paper or white index stock paper
- one popsicle stick
- 9" x 12" light blue construction paper for background page
- glue, glue stick, or paste
- scissors
- pencil and crayons
- transparent tape (optional)
- caption rectangle reading "Oo is for octagon, like a stop sign."
- one language bubble

Directions

1. Direct the students to cut out the caption rectangle reading "Oo is for octagon . . ." and glue it to the top of the light blue background page. On the lower half of the background page, the students draw or color a street scene, including the street and a car. They may also want to include buildings as part of their pictures. The students must include someone or something in their picture that can be the subject for the language bubble. This might be a person in the car, a person on the street, or an animal.
2. When the street scene is complete, the students color and cut out the blackline master of the octagon (the stop sign). The popsicle stick will serve as the post for the stop sign and is glued or taped to the back of the octagon. The stop sign is glued to the street scene.
3. Finally, students glue the language bubble to an appropriate spot in the picture.

Pp Is For Pattern On This Shirt Of Mine

Materials

Each child will need:
- blackline master of tee-shirt, reproduced or traced on white construction paper or heavy index stock paper
- 9½" x 7½" sheet of white or manila paper
- 9" x 12" orange construction paper for background page
- glue, glue stick, or paste
- scissors
- pencil and crayons
- caption rectangle reading "Pp is for pattern on this shirt of mine."
- one language bubble

If the students have not studied about patterns in math, the teacher will need to conduct a lesson on patterns. Patterns can be identified in the room, on the students' clothing, etc. The students should be given an opportunity to make patterns using manipulatives, such as various colored milk caps, buttons, colored blocks, colored plastic clothespins, etc.

Directions

1. Direct the students to cut out the caption rectangle reading "Pp is for pattern . . ." and glue it to the top of the orange background page.
2. The students then need to color the stripes on the tee-shirt on the blackline master, cut it out, and glue it to the center of the 9½" x 7½" sheet of white or manila paper.
3. The students then draw or color a person wearing the tee-shirt, adding a head, arms, legs, feet, etc. After the person is complete, instruct each student to cut it out and glue it to the orange background page.
4. Finally, students add to the picture the language bubble.

Qq Is For Quilt, A Cover On My Bed

Materials

Each child will need:
- blackline master of quilt, reproduced or traced on white construction paper
- eight 1¼" squares of yellow construction paper (or any other color)
- eight 1¼" squares of green construction paper (or any other color)
- 9" x 12" royal blue construction paper for background page
- glue, glue stick, or paste
- scissors
- pencil and crayons
- caption rectangle reading "Qq is for quilt, a cover on my bed."
- one language bubble

This activity also focuses on patterns. The students will be asked to make a pattern on their quilt from the 1¼" colored squares of construction paper.

Directions

1. Direct the students to cut out the caption rectangle reading "Qq is for quilt . . ." and glue it to the top of the blue background page. Afterwards, the students need to color the bed and the outside edges of the quilt on the blackline master. The pillow should remain white so that a face can be drawn or colored in that area.
2. The entire picture can then be cut out and glued to the blue background page.
3. The students begin making a pattern on the quilt by choosing two colors from the 1¼" squares and alternating the position of the squares.
4. Finally, students add to the picture the language bubble.

Rr Is For Robot With A Square Head

Materials

Each child will need:
- a variety of pre-cut geometric shapes which have been cut from discarded wallpaper samples, or cardboard geometric shapes used to trace shapes onto wallpaper (see blackline master for suggested geometric shapes to use as patterns)
- black permanent felt-tip marker
- 9" x 12" red construction paper for background page
- glue, glue stick, or paste
- scissors
- pencil and crayons
- caption rectangle reading "Rr is for robot with a square head."
- one language bubble

Directions

1. Provide the students with a variety of geometric shapes which have been cut from wallpaper scraps. Wallpaper stores often give away discarded books of wallpaper samples. For this activity, wallpaper with designs on silver backgrounds works best. Students should select enough shapes to form a robot. The shapes are to be glued to the red background page in any robot design the students wish. The only stipulation is that each robot have a square head.
2. (Option) The teacher may want students to cut out their own geometric shapes. If this is the case, the teacher needs to trace the blackline master geometric shapes onto cardboard or posterboard, cut them out, and have the cardboard shapes available for the students to trace onto wallpaper.
3. After the robots have been created, students can color a face and other designs on their robots with a black marker. The teacher may want to provide old tee-shirts or painting smocks for the students to wear while using the black markers.
4. The caption rectangle, "Rr is for robot . . ." is cut out and added to the top of the red background page, and a language bubble is glued in an appropriate place.

Ss Is For Stars That Twinkle At Night

Materials

Each child will need:
- ten ½" and one 1" "peel and stick" or gummed foil gold and silver stars
- 9" x 12" white construction paper for background page
- blue tempera paint (slightly watered-down)
- paintbrush
- glue, glue stick, or paste
- scissors
- pencil and crayons
- caption rectangle reading "Ss is for stars that twinkle at night."
- one language bubble

This activity involves making a crayon resistant picture.

Directions

1. Direct the students to color a picture of a house with trees and grass, or any outdoor scene, on the lower half of the white background page. It is essential that they press very hard with their crayons and cover all areas of their picture. For instance, if they color a house, they must color, pressing hard, all of the roof, walls, etc., and not leave any white spaces. It is important that the scene have colored grass or ground so that, when painted, the ground does not turn blue with paint. The focal point of this picture will be the stars in the sky, so stress to the students to leave plenty of room for the sky.

2. After the students have completed their pictures, they will paint the entire page with watered-down blue tempera paint. When applying the paint to the picture, stroke very lightly with the brush across the surface of the page. Everything that was left uncolored will soak up the blue paint, and the wax from the colored areas will resist most of the paint.

3. When the paint is dry, direct the students to cut out the caption rectangle reading "Ss is for stars . . ." and glue it to the top of the white background page. The students then stick the stars to various spots in the sky. If any stars tend not to stick, apply glue. The large star can have the language bubble directed toward it.

Tt Is For Teeth That Are Healthy And White

Materials

Each child will need:
- blackline master of the teeth, reproduced on 8½" x 11" white paper
- 9" x 12" green construction paper for background page
- glue, glue stick, or paste
- scissors
- pencil and crayons
- caption rectangle reading "Tt is for teeth that are healthy and white."
- one language bubble

When reproducing the blackline master of the teeth, position the picture of the teeth just slightly below the center of the page. Each child will need one sheet of white paper that has teeth photocopied on it.

Directions

1. Direct the students to cut out the caption rectangle reading "Tt is for teeth . . ." and glue it to the top of the green background page.
2. Then have the students draw or color a face and head around the picture of the teeth on the sheet of white paper.
3. When the face is complete, the students should cut it out and glue it to the green background page.
4. Finally, students add to the picture the language bubble.

Uu Is For Umbrella You Hold Above Your Head

Materials

Each child will need:
- blackline master of the umbrella, reproduced or traced on white construction paper or index stock paper
- 4" segment of black pipe cleaner
- 9" x 12" light blue construction paper for background page
- glue, glue stick, or paste
- scissors
- transparent tape (optional)
- pencil and crayons
- caption rectangle reading "Uu is for umbrella you hold above your head."
- one language bubble

Directions

1. Direct the students to cut out the caption rectangle reading "Uu is for umbrella . . ." and glue it to the top of the light blue background page.
2. The students color the umbrella from the blackline master and cut it out.
3. The pipe cleaner is bent at one end to form a "U" shape. It will serve as the umbrella's handle. The other end of the pipe cleaner is glued or taped to the backside of the paper umbrella.
4. Have students draw a person in the middle of the blue background page. This person will eventually hold the umbrella. They may want to color clouds, raindrops, rain puddles, etc., on their picture.
5. After completing their drawings, the students glue the umbrella and handle to the picture.
6. A language bubble is glued in an appropriate place.

Vv Is For Vase With Flowers Yellow And Red

Materials

Each child will need:

- blackline master of the vase, reproduced or traced on royal blue or purple construction paper
- 9" x 12" light blue construction paper for background page
- yellow and red tempera paint
- two small sponges
- two clothespins to hold sponges
- glue, glue stick, or paste
- scissors
- pencil and crayons
- caption rectangle reading "Vv is for vase with flowers yellow and red."
- one language bubble

This activity involves sponge painting the yellow and red flowers in the vase. For an explanation of clothespin sponge painting, refer to page 34.

Directions

1. Direct the students to cut out the caption rectangle reading "Vv is for vase . . ." and glue it to the top of the light blue background page.
2. Next, the students use crayons to decorate the royal blue, or purple, vase from the blackline master, cut it out, and glue it to the light blue background page. When gluing the vase, direct the students to center it on the page with the bottom edge of the vase approximately ¼" from the bottom edge of the background page.
3. The students use a green crayon to color stems with leaves at the top of the vase. With any color crayon, they also color a bug (a ladybug is simple to draw) on the lower right-hand side of the vase. The language bubble can be glued and directed toward the bug.
4. Each student then sponge-paints red and yellow flowers on top of the green stems. Stress to students that they should not cover the caption rectangle with paint. It should also be stressed not to mix the red and yellow paint to make orange. The picture should match the text in the caption rectangle.

Ww Is For Watermelon—This Slice Is For Me

Materials

Each child will need:
- blackline masters of the watermelon slices, reproduced or traced on green and red construction paper
- 6 or 7 watermelon seeds, or a black felt-tip marker
- 8½" x 9½" sheet of white or manila construction paper (for face)
- 8½" x 11" sheet of white or manila construction paper (for hands)
- 9" x 12" purple construction paper for background page
- glue, glue stick, or paste
- scissors
- pencil and crayons
- caption rectangle reading "Ww is for watermelon. This slice is for me."
- one language bubble

Directions

1. Direct the students to cut out the caption rectangle reading, "Ww is for watermelon . . ." and glue it to the top of the purple background page.
2. Students then draw or color a face on the 8½" x 9½" sheet of white or manila construction paper. Stress that the face should fill up most of the page. Also discuss with the students how a person's mouth would be open when biting a piece of watermelon and that they should draw their face's mouth open.
3. After drawing the face, students color it, cut it out, and glue it to the purple background page, leaving enough room at the bottom of the page for the watermelon slice.
4. The students now trace their hands onto the 8½" x 11" sheet of white or manila construction paper. The traced hands are colored, cut out, and placed aside.
5. The watermelon slices from the blackline master are then cut from red and green construction paper. The red slice is centered and glued on top of the green slice so that the top horizontal lines of both slices are evenly lined up.
6. The cut-out hands are folded in half across the palms and the watermelon slice placed inside the hands so that it appears that the hands are holding the watermelon. If the fingers cover up too much of the watermelon, pull each cut-out hand back slightly so that more of the red of the watermelon can be seen.
7. Glue is applied beneath the hands' fingertips and glued to the face, positioned slightly below the top of the mouth.
8. Watermelon seeds are glued on the red part of the watermelon slice. If seeds are unavailable, students can use a black felt-tip marker to color them in.
9. Finally, a language bubble is added to the picture.

Xx Is For X-Ray Of Bones You Can See

Materials

Each child will need:
- photocopy of x-ray, reproduced from the blackline master, cut out and ready to glue
- 9" x 12" pink construction paper for background page
- glue, glue stick, or paste
- scissors
- pencil and crayons
- caption rectangle reading "Xx is for x-ray of bones you can see."
- one language bubble

Directions

1. Direct the students to cut out the caption rectangle reading "Xx is for x-ray . . ." and glue it to the top of the pink background page.
2. Then students glue the x-ray square to the center of the background page.
3. The students draw or color a person behind the x-ray, adding a head, arms, and legs.
4. A language bubble is added to the picture.

Yy Is For Yo-Yo On A String That Is Blue

Materials

Each child will need:
- blackline master of the yo-yo, reproduced or traced on yellow construction paper
- 10" segment of blue yarn
- 9" x 6" piece of white or manila construction paper
- 9" x 12" light blue construction paper for background page
- glue, glue stick, or paste
- scissors
- pencil and crayons
- transparent tape
- caption rectangle reading "Yy is for yo-yo on a string that is blue."
- one language bubble

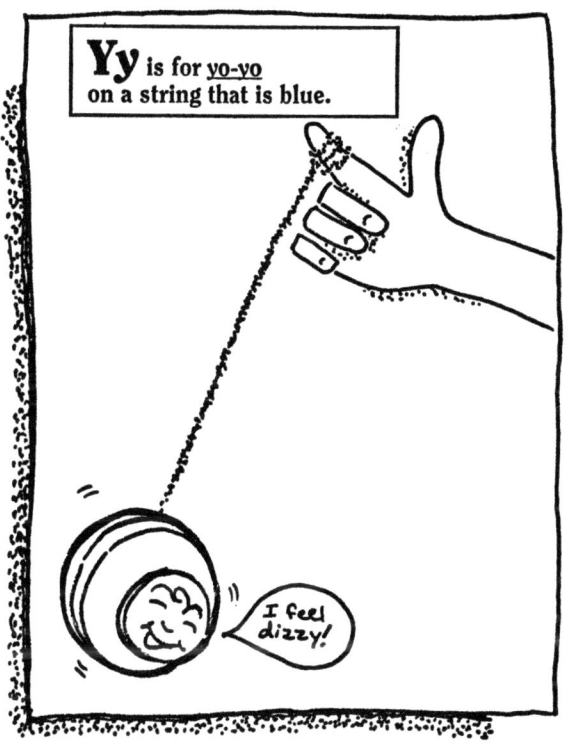

Directions

1. Direct the students to cut out the caption rectangle reading "Yy is for yo-yo . . ." and glue it to the top of the light blue background page.
2. Then students trace their hand and a short section of their wrist onto the 9" x 6" piece of white or manila construction paper, color it, and cut it out. The thumb and index finger of the cut-out hand should remain straight, while the other three fingers are folded against the palm of the hand.
3. Students wrap one end of the blue yarn around the index finger several times. It is a good idea to tape the yarn to the back side of the finger.
4. Students glue the hand on the upper right-hand side of the background page, beneath the caption.
5. Students then color a face on the inside circle of the yo-yo, cut out the yo-yo, and place it on the lower left-hand corner of the background page. Tell the students not to use any glue yet. The loose end of the yarn should be glued or taped to the back of the yo-yo so that the yarn stretches at a diagonal line from the hand to the yo-yo. When this is done, the yo-yo should be glued in place.
6. A language bubble is added to complete the activity.

Zz Is For Zebra You See At The Zoo

Materials

Each child will need:
- one 6" x 9" piece of white tagboard or white index stock paper with student's name printed on back
- cardboard pattern of the zebra to trace (from blackline master)
- black acrylic craft paint (approximately 6 oz. for entire class)
- an empty 4 oz. squeeze-bottle of glue (only one needed for entire class)
- cut segments of "baby" rickrack (one 2½" segment and three 1" segments)
- one small plastic moving eye, purchased at a craft store (optional)
- 9" x 12" light blue construction paper for background page
- glue, glue stick, or paste
- scissors
- pencil and crayons
- caption rectangle reading "Zz is for zebra you see at the zoo."
- one language bubble

Acrylic paint is being used in this art activity instead of tempera paint as tempera paint has a tendency to chip when it is applied too thickly.

Directions

1. The teacher will need to make several cardboard patterns of the zebra from the blackline master, pour the acrylic craft paint into a clean, empty glue bottle (to be used to make the stripes for the zebra), and cover the tabletop of the painting area with newspaper. Students should also have access to old tee-shirts or painting smocks.
2. Students take turns squeezing stripes onto their zebras. This is done by placing the tip of the bottle at the top of the white tagboard card, squeezing gently, and slowly moving the bottle to the bottom of the card. It does not matter if the lines of paint are crooked. If fact, the stripes look more like those of a zebra if they are not all straight. The lines should be made approximately ½" apart across the white card. Allow the paint to dry thoroughly.
3. The striped cards are turned over, and the zebra pattern is traced onto the backs of the cards, then cut out and set aside.
4. Students then cut out the caption rectangle and glue it to the top of the blue background page. Below the caption, the students can color a grassy area in which the zebra lives.
5. The cut-out zebra is then glued to the background page. The 2½" rickrack is added for its mane, and the three 1" segments are added for its tail.
6. Students can use a black marker to draw the zebra's hooves, mouth, and nose. For the zebra's eye, students can either use a marker or glue on a plastic eye, if available.
7. Finally, students add a language bubble to the picture.

Part Three

Blackline Masters
Picture Patterns
Caption Rectangles
Language Bubbles
Cover Page For Student Books

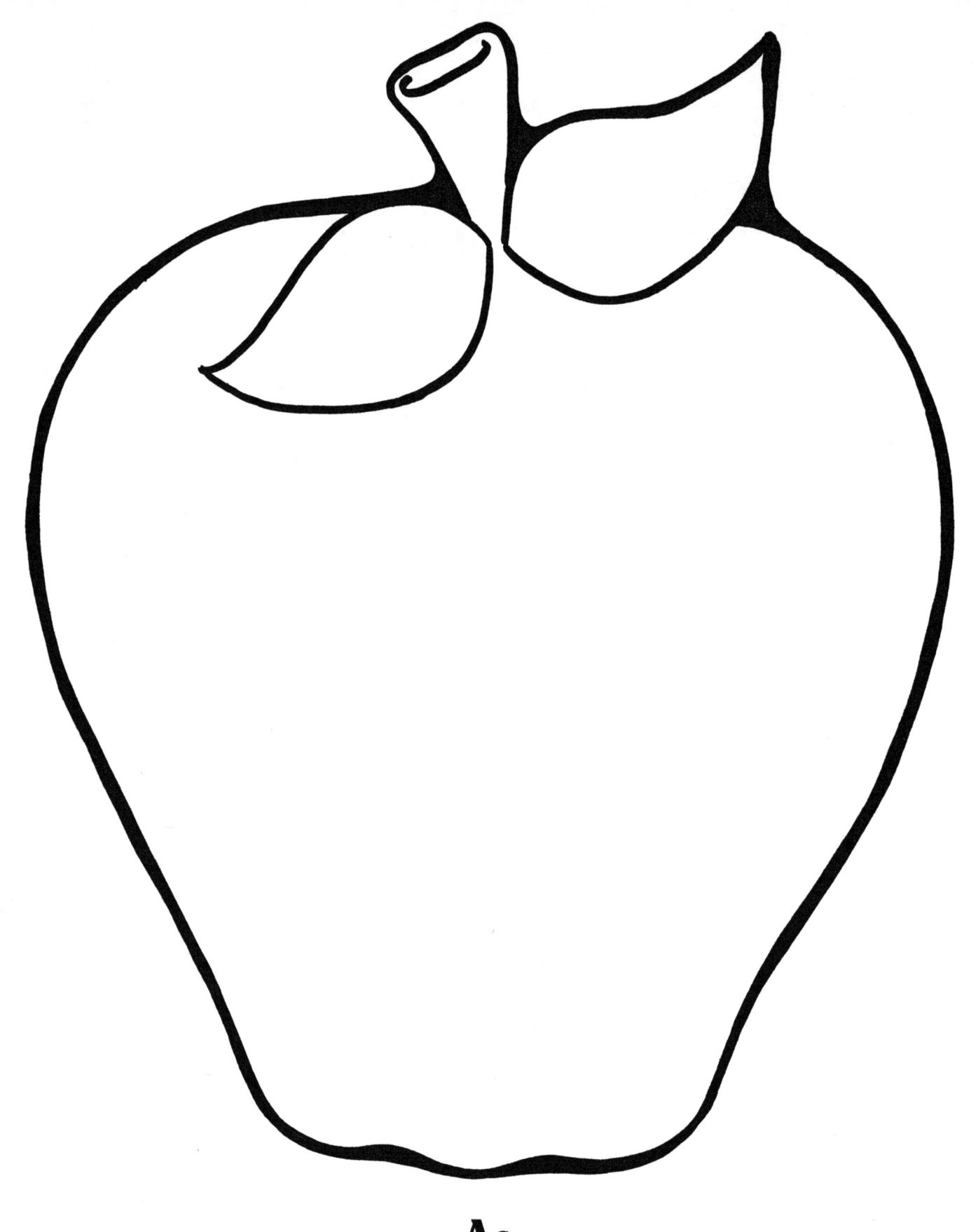

Aa
apple
(reproduce on white paper)

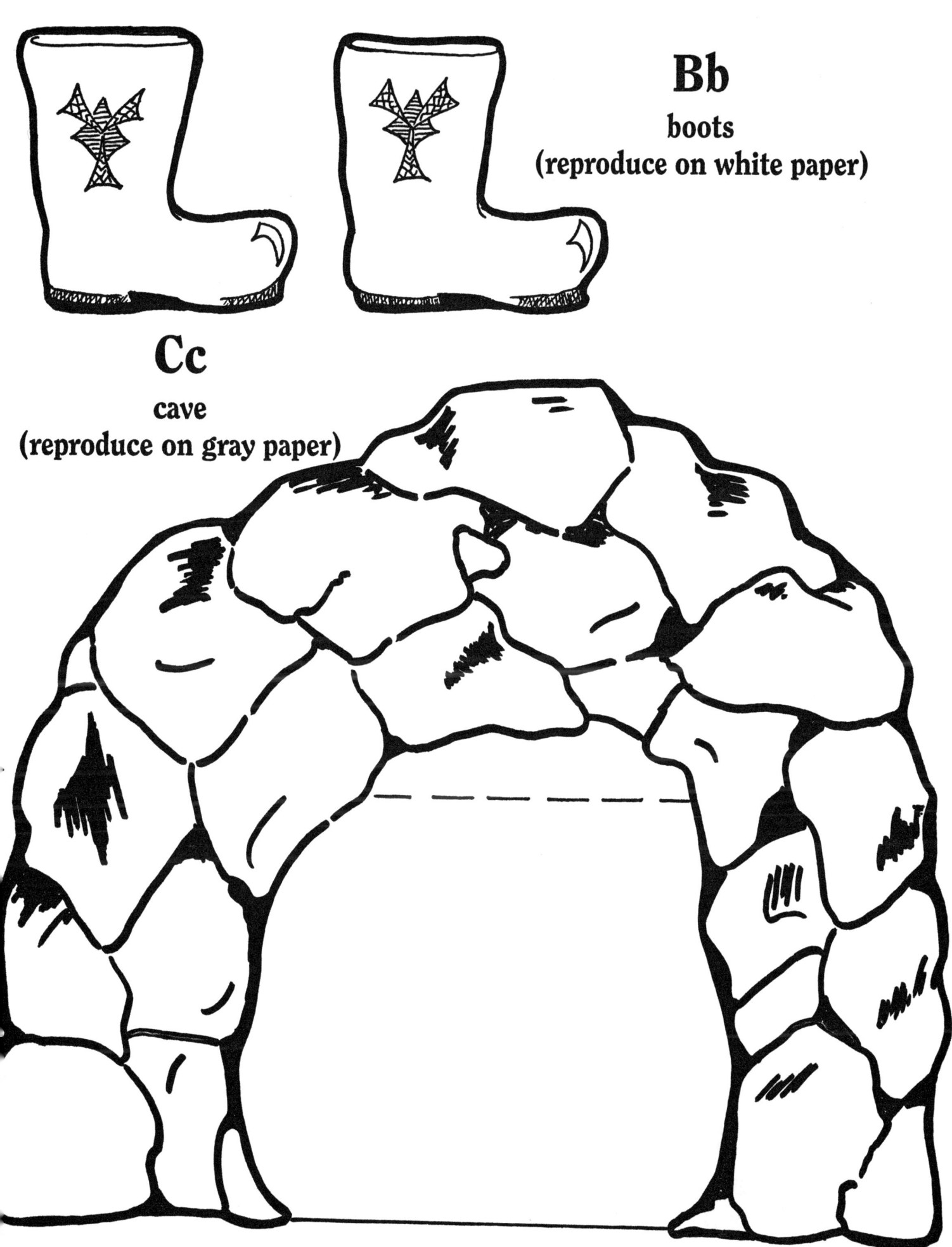

Dd
door
(reproduce on white paper)

Ee
envelope
(use a 3⅝" x 6½" envelope)

© 1995 by Incentive Publications, Inc., Nashville, TN.

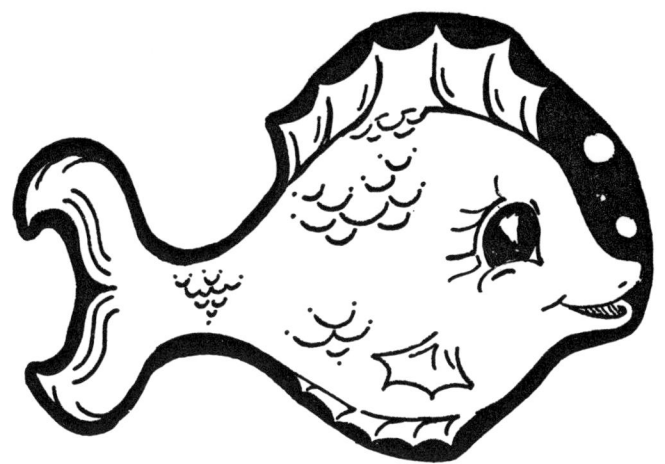

Ff
fish
(reproduce on orange paper)

boat
(reproduce on brown paper)

Gg
gift
(Use this shape to make a pattern for tracing wrapping paper.)

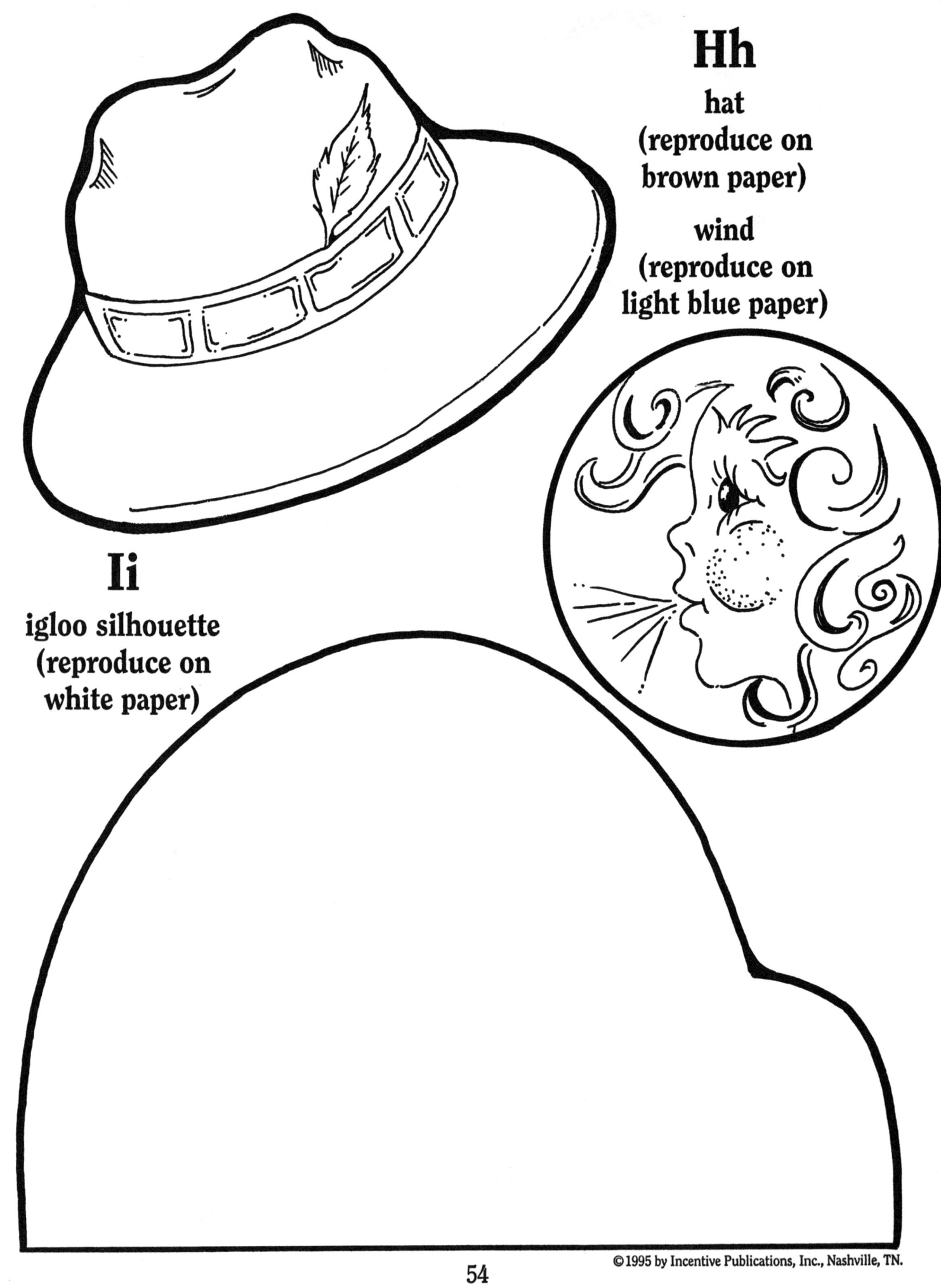

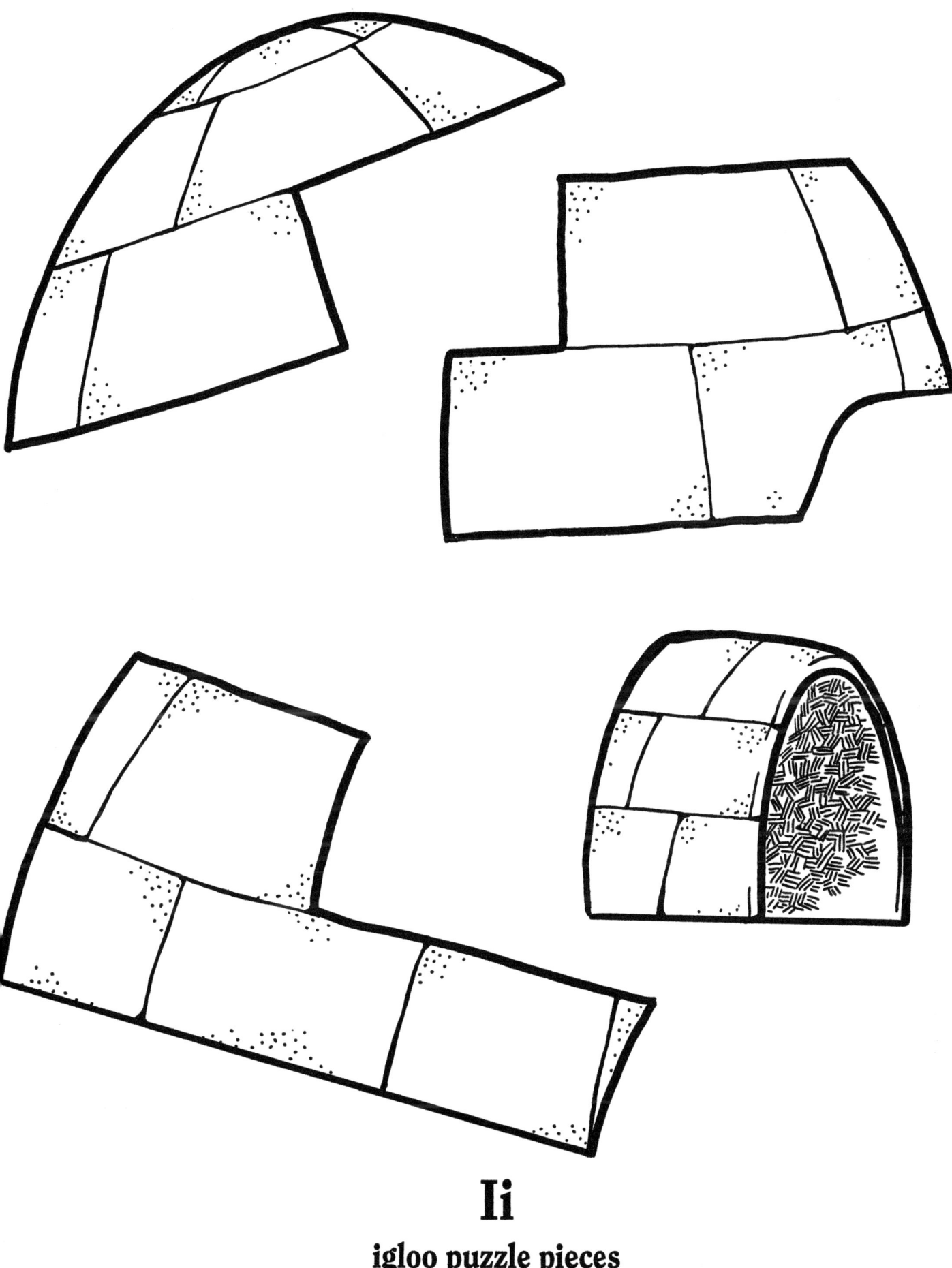

Ii
igloo puzzle pieces
(reproduce on white paper)

Jj
jumping jack box
(reproduce on white paper)

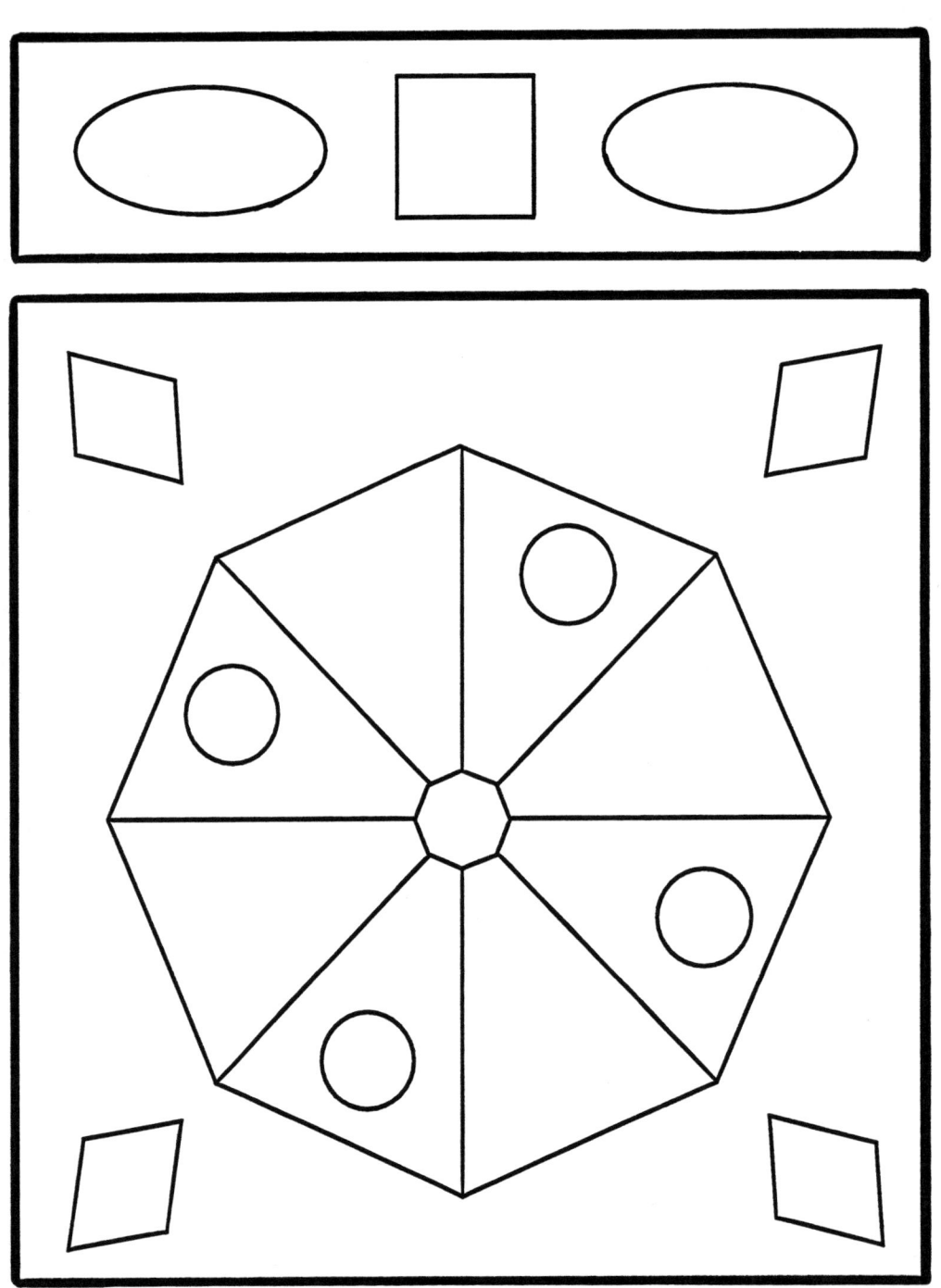

Jj
jumping jack pieces
(reproduce on white paper)

©1995 by INCENTIVE PUBLICATIONS, Inc., Nashville, TN.

Kk
kindergarten

(This name grid is for student signatures. You may need to reduce the size of the signatures after the students have printed their names in order to have room on the red background page for faces and names.)

©1995 by Incentive Publications, Inc., Nashville, TN.

Kk
king
for first and second grades
(reproduce on yellow paper)

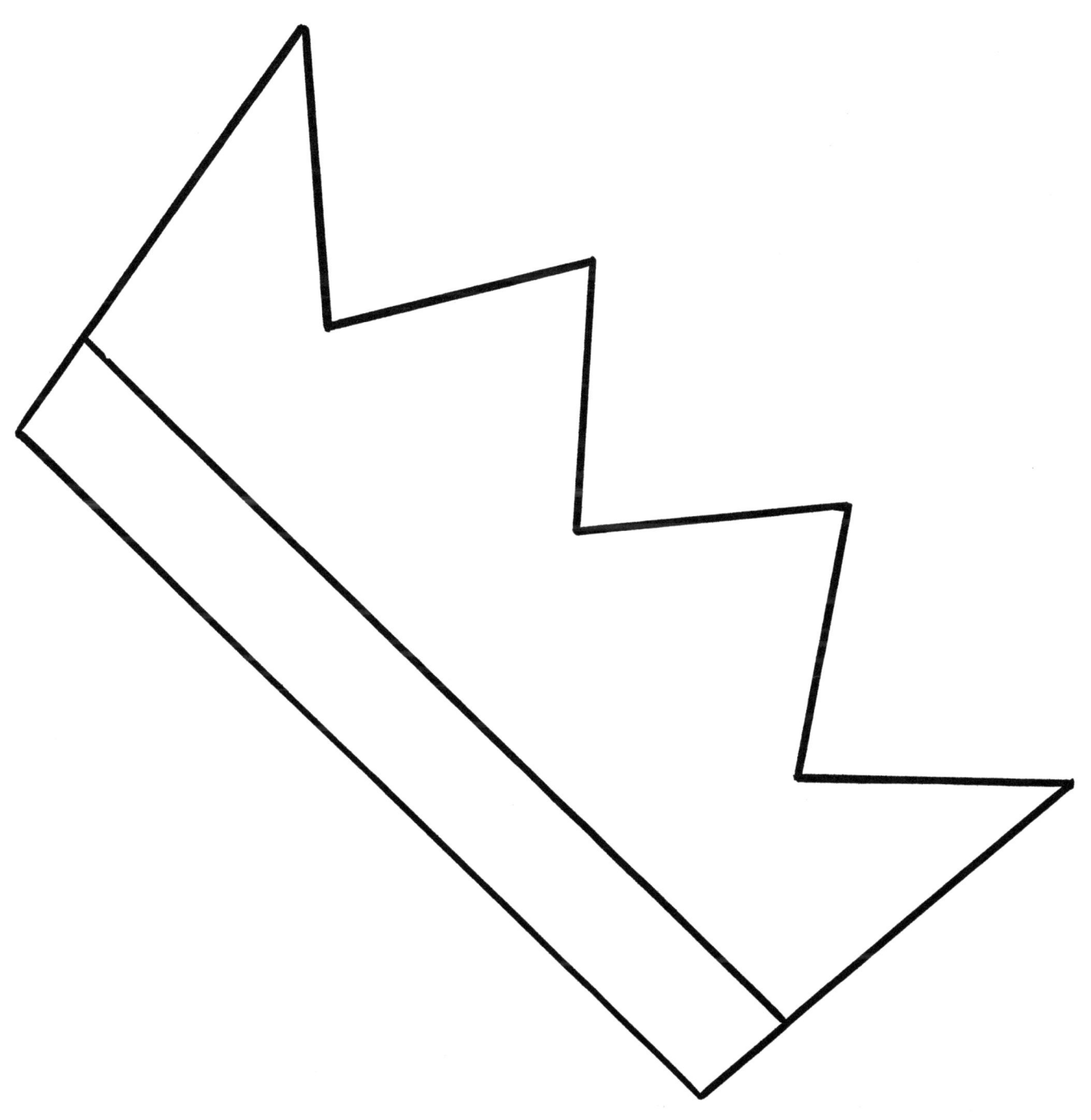

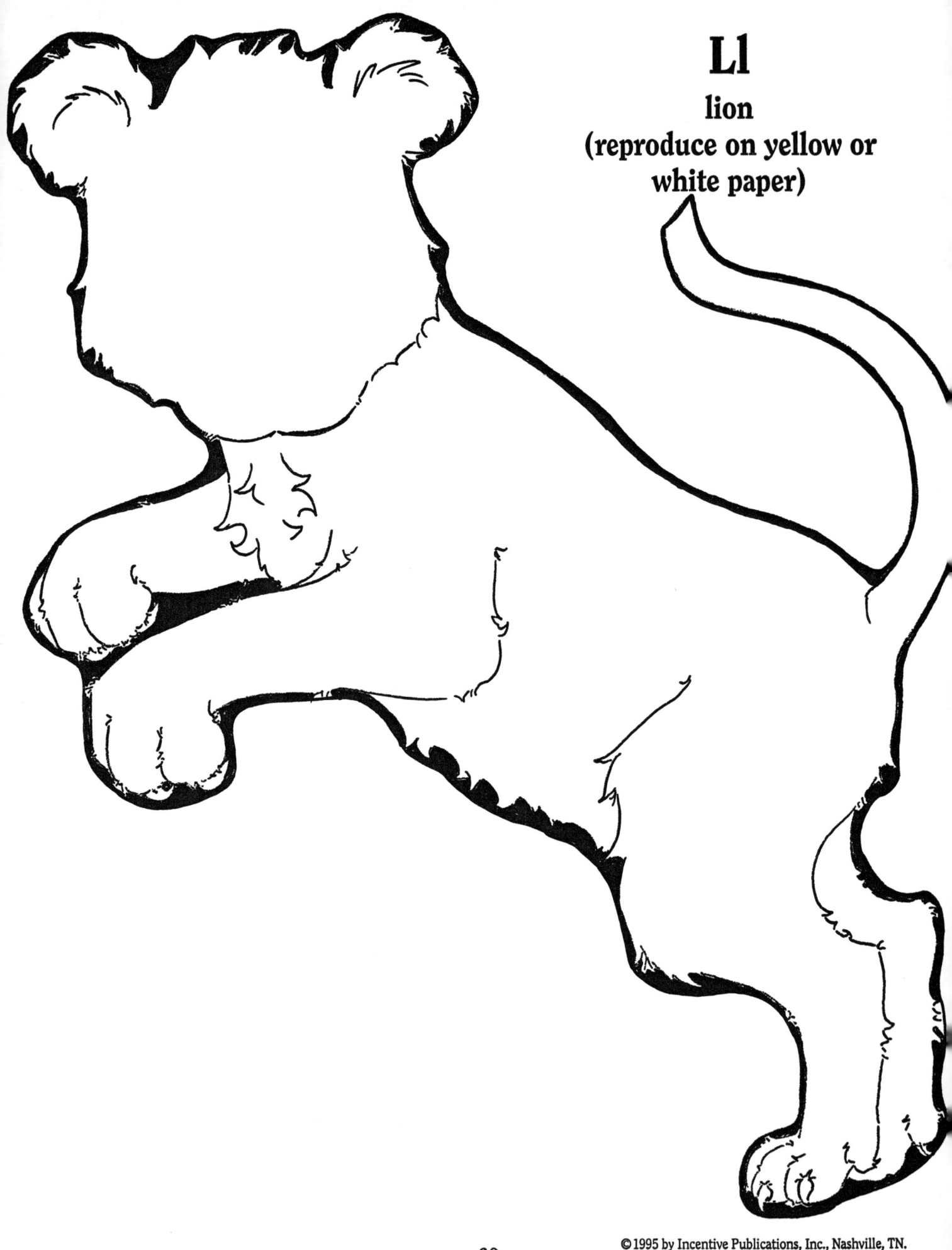

Ll
lion
(reproduce on yellow or white paper)

©1995 by Incentive Publications, Inc., Nashville, TN.

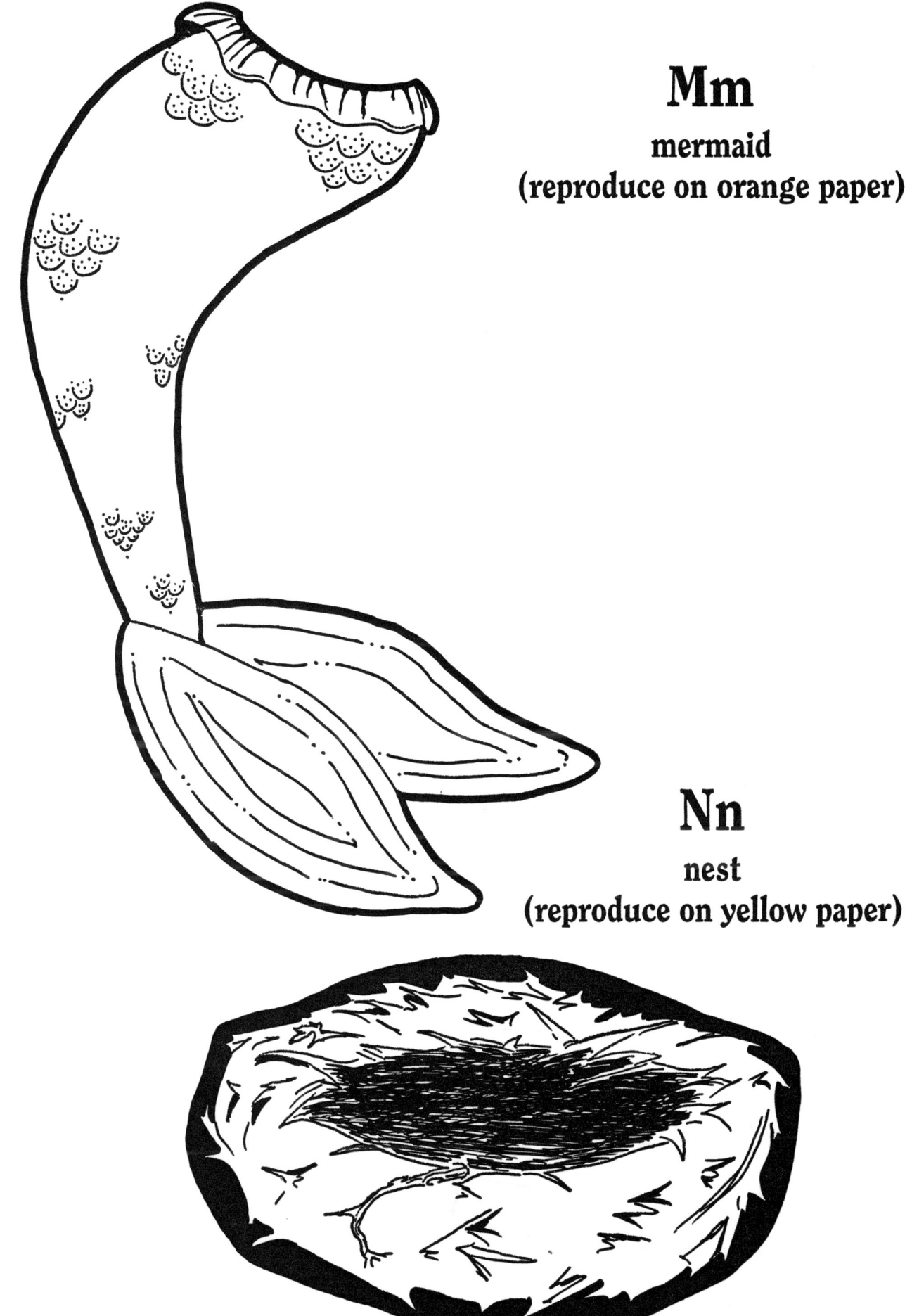

Mm
mermaid
(reproduce on orange paper)

Nn
nest
(reproduce on yellow paper)

Oo
octagon
(reproduce on white paper)

Pp
pattern
(reproduce on white paper)

Qq
quilt (reproduce on white paper)

Ss
stars
(Use commercially-made "peel and stick" or gummed gold and silver stars in ½" and 1" sizes.)

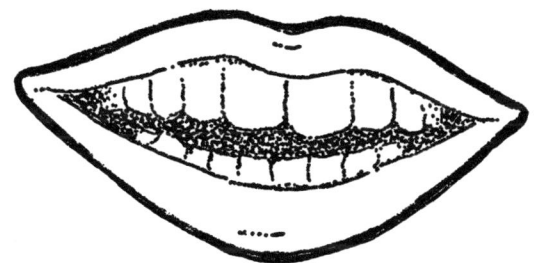

Tt
teeth
(reproduce on white paper)

Uu
umbrella
(reproduce on white paper)

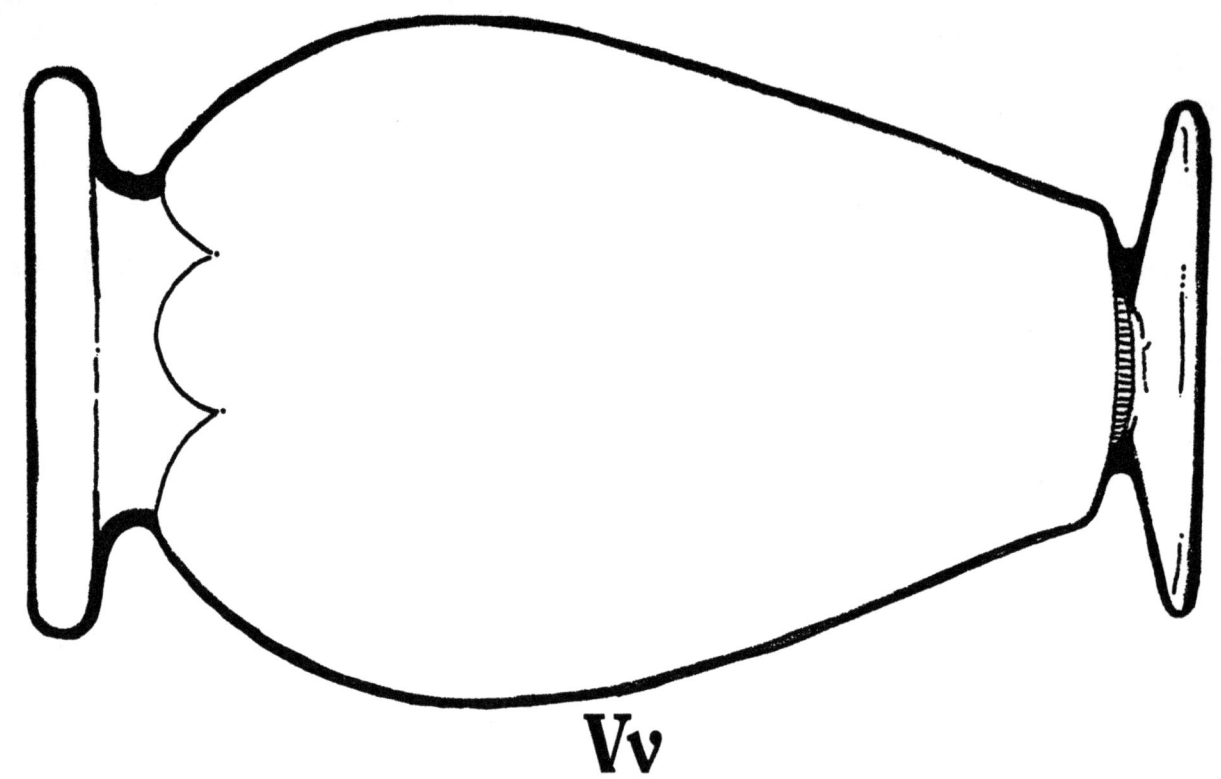

Vv

vase
(reproduce on royal blue or purple paper)

Ww

watermelon
(reproduce on green paper)

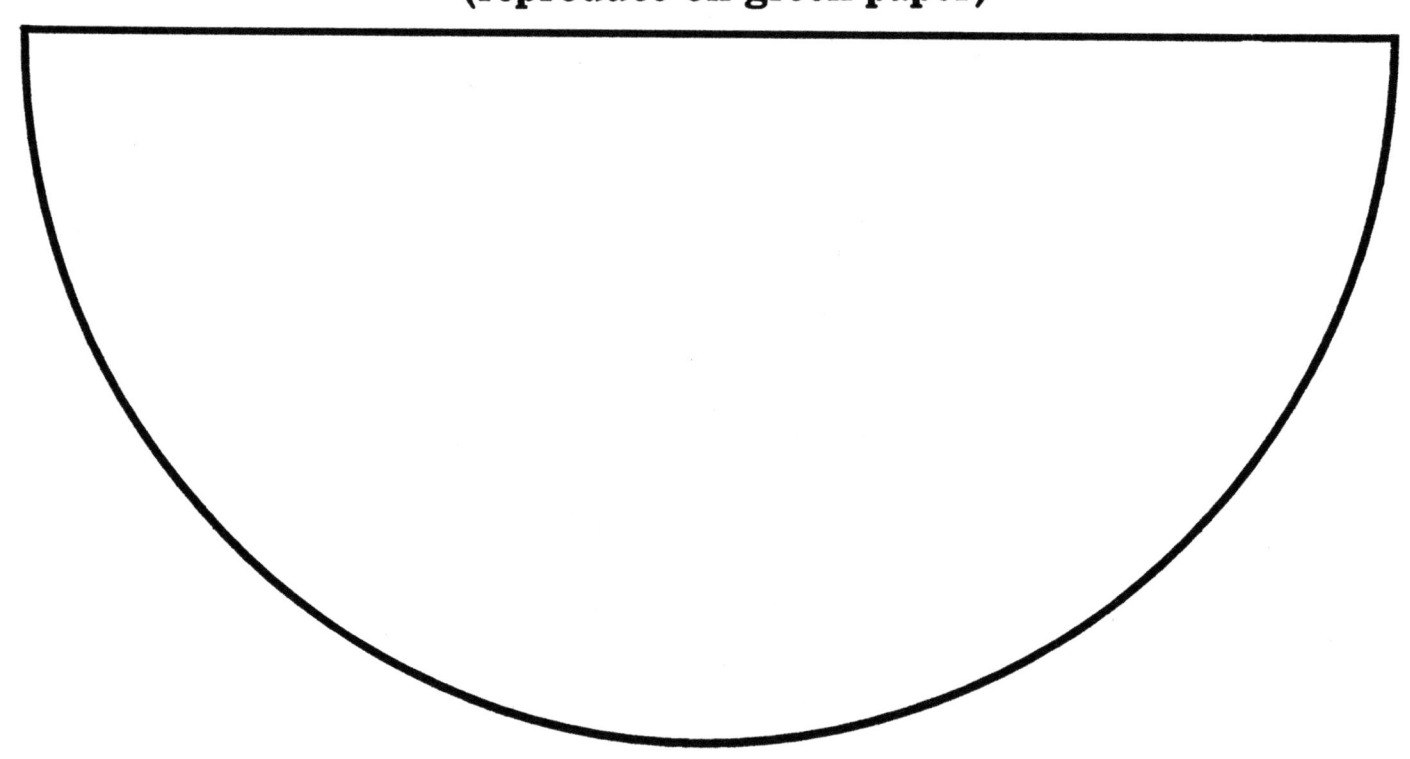

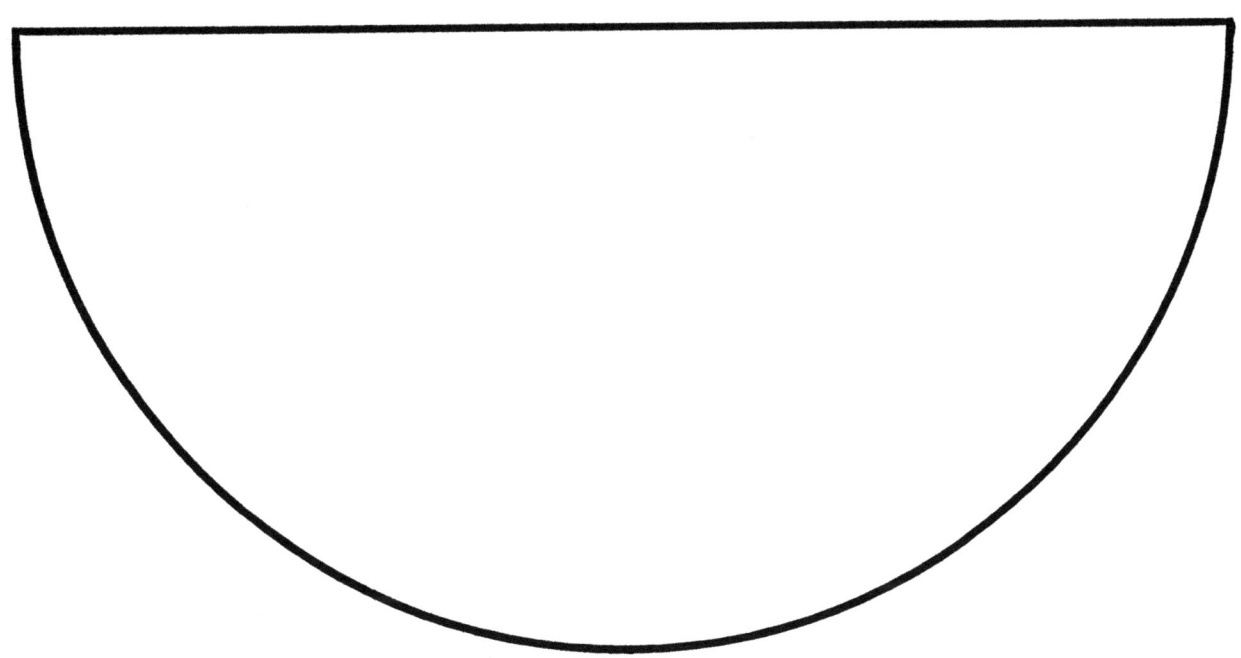

Ww

**watermelon
(reproduce on red paper)**

Xx

**x-ray
(reproduce on white paper)**

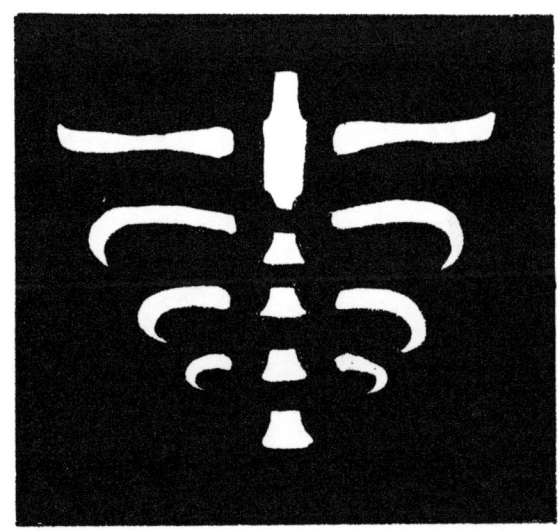

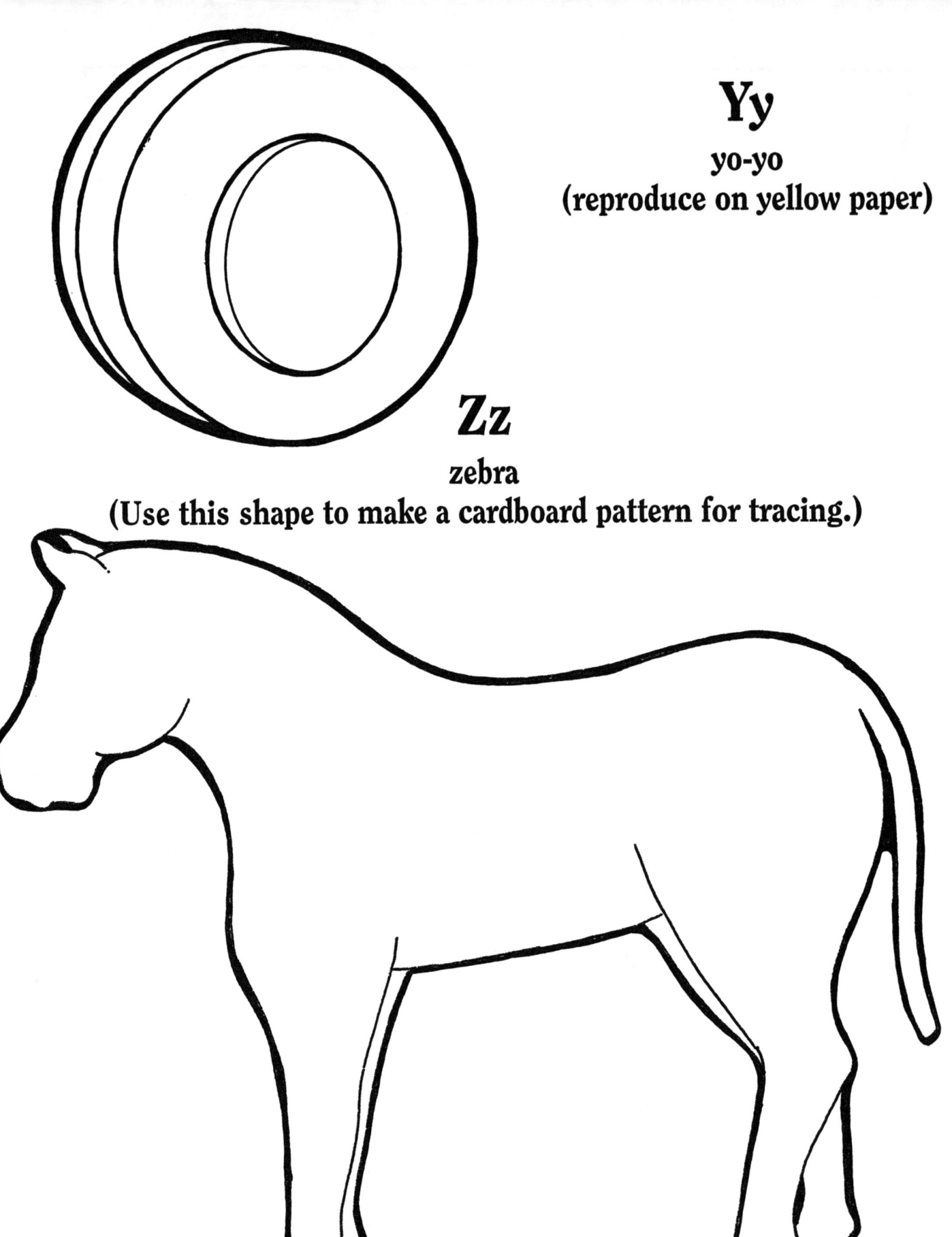

Yy
yo-yo
(reproduce on yellow paper)

Zz
zebra
(Use this shape to make a cardboard pattern for tracing.)

©1995 by Incentive Publications, Inc., Nashville, TN.

Caption Rectangles

(reproduce on white paper)

Aa is for <u>apple</u>,
juicy and sweet.

Bb is for <u>boots</u>
you wear on your feet.

Cc is for <u>cave</u>,
a home for a bear.

Dd is for <u>door</u>.
Knock, knock, who's there?

Ee is for <u>envelope</u>.
Inside is a note.

Ff is for <u>fish</u>,
swimming under the boat.

Gg is for <u>giving</u> a <u>gift</u>
to a friend.

Hh is for <u>hat</u>
that blows off in the wind.

Ii is for <u>igloo</u>
made of icy snow blocks.

Jj is for <u>jumping jack</u>
who lives in a box.

Kk is for <u>kindergarten</u>
with kids all around.

Kk is for <u>king</u>
with a crown made of gold.

Ll is for <u>lion</u>
that leaps with a bound.

Ll is for <u>lion</u>
that is fierce and bold.

Mm is for <u>mermaid</u>
who swims in the sea.

Nn is for <u>nest</u>
on the branch of a tree.

Oo is for <u>octagon</u>, like a stop sign.

Pp is for <u>pattern</u> on this shirt of mine.

Qq is for <u>quilt</u>, a cover on my bed.

Rr is for <u>robot</u> with a square head.

Ss is for <u>stars</u>
that twinkle at night.

Tt is for <u>teeth</u>
that are healthy and white.

Uu is for <u>umbrella</u>
you hold above your head.

Vv is for <u>vase</u>
with flowers yellow and red.

Ww is for watermelon.
This slice is for me.

Xx is for x-ray
of bones you can see.

Yy is for yo-yo
on a string that is blue.

Zz is for zebra
you see at the zoo.

©1995 by Incentive Publications, Inc., Nashville, TN.

Language Bubbles

It is recommended that the teacher have the language bubbles pre-cut and stored in a small container, ready for student use. These can be reproduced on white paper.

Cover Page For Student Books

Materials

Each child will need:
- cover page (see page 78) reproduced on 8½" x 11" sheet of yellow paper
- two 9" x 12" sheets of green construction paper
- crayons
- close-up photo of child's face (optional)
- language bubble (optional)

Children should color their cover page after completing all 26 alphabet-art activities. When this is the final step in completing the book, children take more time and pride in completing the activity.

Directions:

1. Direct the children to color the apples and ribbons on the yellow cover page. They should also be directed to write their names on the back of the page.

   An adult should complete the following steps to finish the cover page.

2. A photo of the child can be taped to the circle on the apple. While this is optional, it does make an attractive cover and provides the child with a sense of ownership. Cut out the circle in the apple and tape the photo to the back of the yellow cover page so that it can be seen in the center of the apple. Add a language bubble to the child's picture and have each child dictate how he or she feels about the book. This, also, is optional. (If a photo is not used, the children can draw or color their faces inside the apple, or the teacher may delete the circle before reproducing it.)
3. Mount the yellow cover sheet on one of the 9" x 12" sheets of green construction paper using glue or rubber cement.
4. Both sheets of green paper should then be laminated or covered with contact paper for durability.

Refer to page 11 for ideas for binding the student books.

Aa Is for Apple

My Alphabet-Art Book

Part Four

Extension Activities

Extension Activities

Center Games

- Use the reduced-size pictures on pages 86–93 to make center games for letter, sound and symbol, and word identification.
- The pictures should be colored, cut out, and mounted on tagboard cards to be matched with the appropriate letter or word.
- They can also be used for a sequencing activity. Instead of placing letter cards in ABC order, let the children place the picture cards in proper order according to the "Aa Is for Apple" song. It will be an excellent opportunity to use the ordinal number words "first" through "twenty-sixth," as well as position words such as "between," "next to," "before," "after," etc.

Concentration

- Use the picture cards on pages 86–93 to play a large- or small-group game of concentration.
- One one side of a pocket chart or designated area of the floor, place the picture cards backwards in a column. On the opposite side, forming a column, place letter or word cards facing backwards.
- The game is played by having a child select a card from the left-hand column, turn it over, and then select a card from the right-hand column and turn it over. If the cards match (picture with letter or word), the cards remain face-up and the children receive a point. If the cards do not match, they must be turned face-down again, and the cards receive a point. Someone can keep a tally on the chalkboard for scoring purposes. This type of game promotes teamwork and doesn't focus on individual competition.
- For a variation of this game, the teacher can make additional picture cards, one for each sound or symbol. When a child turns over a picture card from the left-hand column, such as a door, he or she must then select and turn over a picture of something from the right-hand column that starts with the same sound, such as dog. If both pictures start with the same sound, it's a match. If not, the cards are turned over and someone else gets a turn.

Guess And Check For Letter Order

- This game can be used in large or small groups.
- Display letter cards in alphabetical sequence along a chalkboard tray. (If your students have not yet mastered letter identification, you may want to also have the picture cards placed next to the letter cards serving as picture clues for letter identification.)
- One child, with back facing the chalk tray, draws a letter card out of a container. The child has a few seconds to name the letter which has been chosen, and then he or she must name the letter in the alphabet that comes before or after that letter. To check the answer, the child turns around, finds the chosen letter on the chalk tray, and sees if his or her answer was correct.

Dramatization/ Letter Identification

- In order to play the following game, the children must know the body movements to the "Aa Is for Apple" song.
- This game can be used in large or small groups.
- Display letter cards on a pocket chart or along the edge of the chalkboard tray. The children should sit facing the letter cards.
- One child is selected to stand before the group to dramatize or act out a chosen letter. He or she does this by first drawing a letter card out of a container. If the child does not know the letter, the teacher may have to whisper it in his or her ear.
- The child now performs the body motions for that given letter and recites the phrase from the "Aa Is for Apple" song. Afterward, he or she calls on a child seated to come up to the chalkboard and find the letter which represents the dramatization. If the child selects the correct letter, he or she gets to be "it" next and dramatize another letter phrase. If the incorrect letter is chosen, the performing child chooses another student until the correct letter is identified.
- For a variation of this game, let the person standing in front of the class be the only one who does not know the "mystery letter" to be acted out. To do this, let the selected person be a king or a queen and wear a simple cardboard crown. A paper clip should be positioned on the front of the crown. The king or queen places the crown on his or her head, and the teacher then inserts a letter card behind the paper clip so that it is positioned on the forehead. The whole class now acts out the letter movements and the king or queen guesses the answer.

Dramatization/ Handwriting Practice

- Follow the idea of the Letter Identification game, but focus on handwriting skills.
- Have the children who are seated guess the letter represented by the dramatization by writing their answers on paper or individual chalkboards. After they have written their answers, they should hold up their papers or chalkboards. The teacher then has the opportunity to discuss and review the correct handwriting formation. It should be decided before beginning the game whether to use capital or lower case letters.
- For a variation of this game, and to focus on letter sequence, have the children write not only the letter being acted out, but also the letters that come before and after.

Dramatization/ Practice Writing Spelling Or Sight Words

- This game should be used with first and second grade students.
- Print spelling or sight words on pieces of paper or cards and place them in a container. The selected words should be simple ones with no more than two or three letters.
- The game is played by having a child, or the teacher, randomly draw a word from the container and act it out, letter by letter. (The teacher may want to act out the first few words until the children feel confident to perform.)
- To act out a word, the performer holds up one finger to represent the first letter in the word (as in a game of Charades). The performer then dramatizes the body movement for this letter from the "Aa Is for Apple" song. The rest of the children write their guess for this letter. The performer continues in this way with the rest of the letters until the entire word has been dramatized. A child is then selected to read the word.

Dramatization

- Brainstorm words that start with the letter/sound being studied. The teacher should write the words on the board as the children think of them.
- Afterwards, the class should read the words as a group as the teacher points to each word.
- A child should now be selected to come to the front of the class to dramatize one of the words on the board using movements they create on the spot. The class should then guess which word is being dramatized. This activity also works to review spelling and sight words.
- For a variation of this activity, have the class brainstorm rhyming words, naming words, action words, or words having a particular vowel sound. After this has been done, select a child to choose a word from the board and creatively act it out. The class then guesses which word on the board has been dramatized.

Quiet Times

Have you ever had to keep the children in your class quiet as they wait in a hallway? Young children often find it difficult to stand and wait quietly. The next time you need to keep your group silent, try this activity.

- Lead the class in a silent singing of "Aa Is for Apple." Silently sing the song while you act out the body movements. You may look strange to other teachers, but at least your students will be quietly entertained as they exercise their brains.

Substitute Folder

Once your class is familiar with the words and body movements of "Aa Is for Apple," you might want to include the dramatization games described above in your substitute folder. When the children are familiar with the games, they serve as excellent activities for a substitute who might need some time-fillers throughout the day.

School Programs Or Skits

Have you ever been asked at the last minute to prepare a class skit or song for a PTA program? Even coming up with something simple can be stressful and time-consuming. Why not let your class sing the "Aa Is for Apple" song and perform the body movements? Some of your students could act out the song while others hold up posters of the letters. You could let the audience know that your class is currently involved in making an alphabet-art book about the song they will sing.

Part Five

Pictures For Classroom Games

The following pictures can be used to make classroom games for alphabet practice. Refer to the ideas listed in the Extension Activities section, pages 79–83.

86

**Kk is for kindergarten.
(for kindergarten classes)**

The teacher may want to use a group photo of the class instead of the above illustration.

**Kk is for king.
(for first and second grades)**

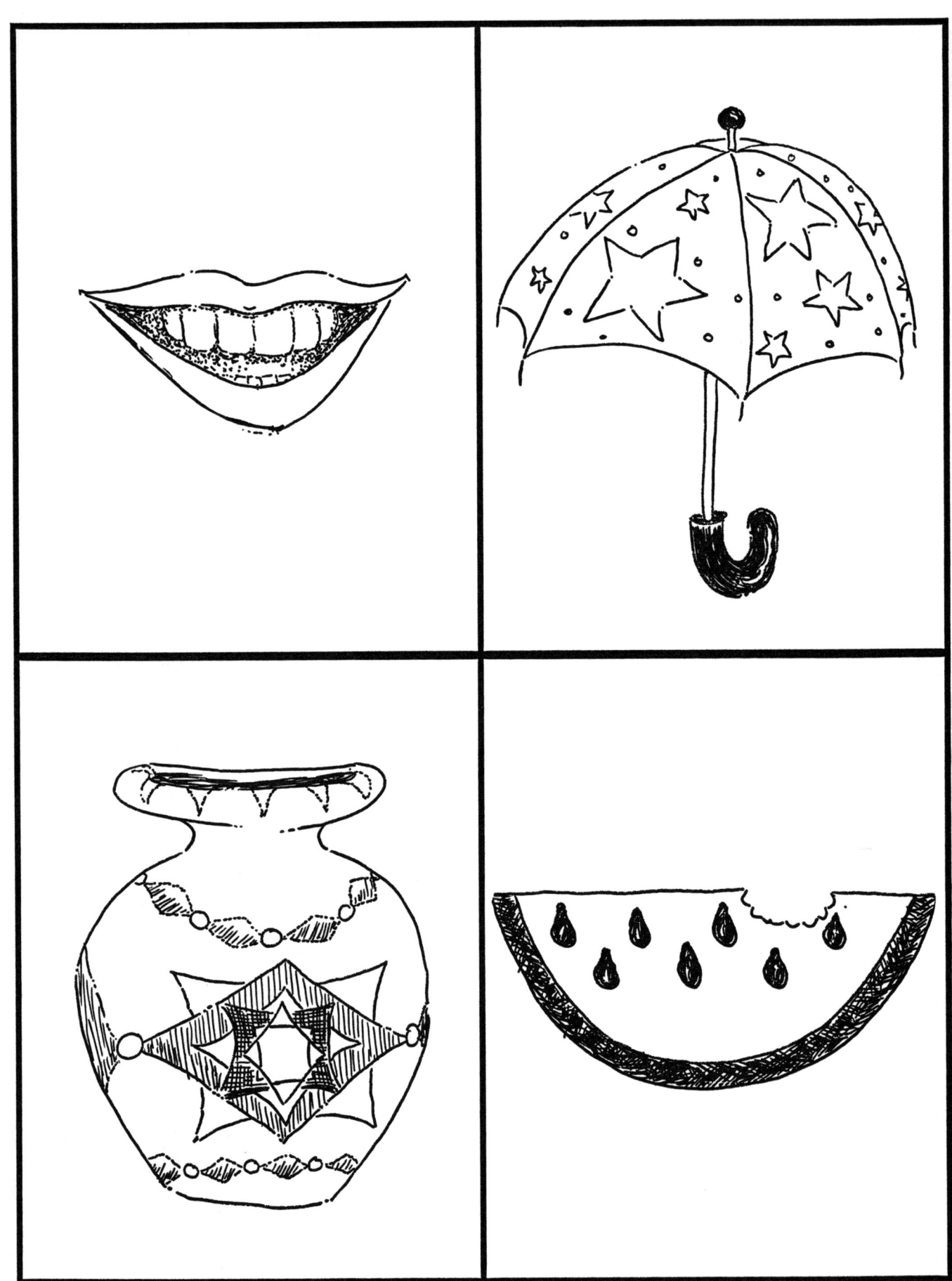

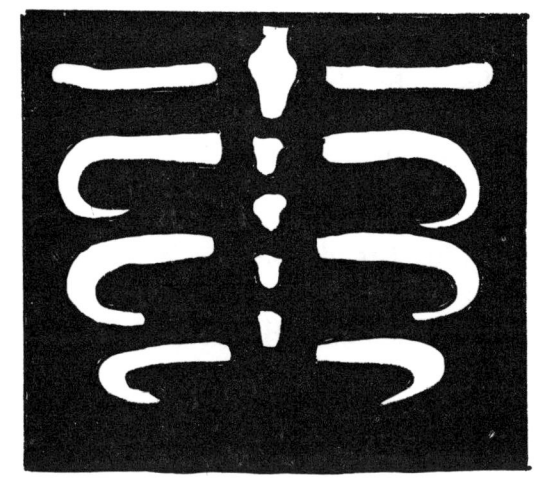
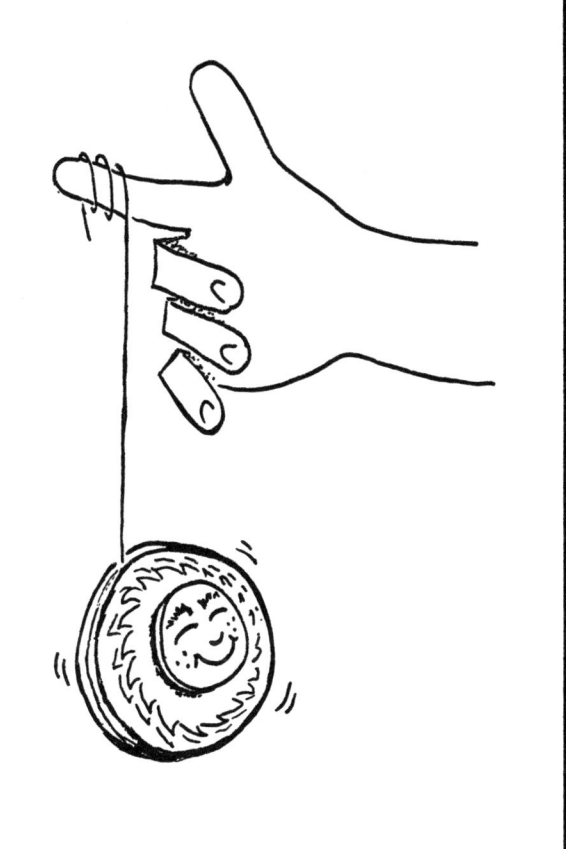

Literature Suggestions To Accompany Activities

Aa Is for Apple
Apple Picking Time by Michele Benoit Slawson. Crown, 1994. Illus. Dehorah Kogan Ray.
Apples by Rhoda Nottridge. Carolrhoda Books, 1991. Illus. John Yates.
Who Stole the Apples? by Sigrid Heuck. Knopf, 1986. Illus. Sigrid Heuck.

Bb Is for Boots
Big Sarah's Little Boots by Paulette Bourgeois. Scholastic, 1987. Illus. Brenda Clark.
Boot Weather by Judith Vigna. Whitman, 1989. Illus. Judith Vigna.
The Magic Boots by Scott Emerson and Howard Post. Gibbs Smith, 1994. Illus. Howard Post.

Cc Is for Cave
Beady Bear by Don Freeman. Viking Press, 1982. Illus. Don Freeman.
The Bear's Cave by Regine Schindler. Dutton, 1990. Illus. Sita Jucker.
Caves and Caverns by Gail Gibbons. Harcourt Brace, 1993. Illus. Gail Gibbons.
Caves by Roma Gans. Crowell, 1976. Illus. Giulio Maestro.

Dd Is for Door
The Doorbell Rang by Pat Hutchins. Greenwillow, 1986. Illus. Pat Hutchins.
Possum Come A-Knockin' by Nancy Van Laan. Knopf, 1990. Illus. George Booth.
Who's That Knocking At My Door? by Tilde Michels. Barron's, 1986. Illus. Reinhard Michl. Translated by Sigrid Brugel and Leslie McGuire.

Ee Is for Envelope
The Jolly Christmas Postman by Janet and Allen Ahlberg. Little, Brown, & Co., 1991. Illus. Janet and Allen Ahlberg.
A Letter To Amy by Ezra Jack Keats. Harper & Row, 1968. Illus. Ezra Jack Keats.

Ff Is for Fish
Fish Is Fish by Leo Lionni. Pantheon Books, 1970. Illus. Leo Lionni.
The Rainbow Fish by Marcus Pfister. North-South Books, 1992. Illus. Marcus Pfister. Translated by J. Alison James.
Swimmy by Leo Lionni. Pantheon Books, 1968. Illus. Leo Lionni.

Gg Is for Giving a Gift
The Birthday Gift That Beeped by Jim Laster. Josten's, 1983. Illus. Julie Erwin. Photographs by David Rogers.
The Christmas Gift by Emily Arnold McCully. Harper & Row, 1988. Illus. Emily Arnold McCully.
The Gift of the Tree by Alvin Tresselt. Lothrop, Lee, & Shepard Books, 1992. Illus. Henri Sorensen.

Hh Is for Hat
Hats, Hats, Hats by Ann Morris. Lothrop, Lee, & Shepard, 1989. Photographs by Ken Heyman.
Jennie's Hat by Ezra Jack Keats. Harper & Row, 1966. Illus. Ezra Jack Keats.
Old Hat, New Hat by Stan and Jan Berenstain. Random House, 1970. Illus. Stan and Jan Berenstain.
The Wind Blew by Pat Hutchins. Macmillan, 1974. Illus. Pat Hutchins.

Ii Is for Igloo
Eskimo Boy by Russ Kendall. Scholastic, 1992. Photographs by Russ Kendall.
Frozen Land, Vanishing Cultures by Jan Reynolds. Harcourt Brace, 1993. Illus. Jan Reynolds.
Mama, Do You Love Me? by Barbara M. Joosse. Chronicle Books, 1991. Illus. Barbara Lavallee.

Jj Is For Jumping Jack
Five Little Monkeys Jumping on the Bed by Eileen Christelow. Clarion Books, 1989. Illus. Eileen Christelow.
Jump, Frog, Jump! by Robert Kalan. Greenwillow Books, 1981. Illus. Byron Barton.
No Jumping on the Bed by Tedd Arnold. Dial Books, 1987. Illus. Tedd Arnold.

Kk Is for Kindergarten and King
All I Really Need To Know I Learned in Kindergarten by Robert Fulghum. G.K. Hall, 1989.
Annabelle Swift, Kindergartner by Amy Schwartz. Orchard Books, 1988. Illus. Amy Schwartz.
King Midas and the Golden Touch by Kathryn Hewitt. Harcourt Brace, 1987. Illus. Kathryn Hewitt.
The King Who Tried To Fry an Egg on His Head by Mirra Ginsburg. Macmillan, 1992. Illus. Will Hillenbrand.

Ll Is for Lion
Dandelion by Don Freeman. Viking Press, 1964. Illus. Don Freeman.
Little Wild Lion Cub by Anna Michel. Pantheon, 1980. Photographs by Tony Chen.
Young Lions by Toshi Yoshida. Philomel Books, 1989. Illus. Toshi Yoshida.

Mm Is for Mermaid
A Book of Mermaids by Ruth Manning-Sanders. Dutton, 1967. Illus. Robin Jacques.
The Little Mermaid by Hans Christian Anderson. Henry Holt and Co., 1993. Illus. by Michael Hague.
Sukey and the Mermaid by Robert D. San Souci. Four Winds Press, 1992. Illus. Brian Pinkney.

Nn Is for Nest
Bird's Nest by Eileen Curran. Troll, 1985. Illus. Pamela Johnson.
A First Look at Bird Nests by Millicent E. Selsam and Joyce Hunt. Walker & Co., 1984. Illus. Harriett Springer.
It's Nesting Time by Roma Gans. Crowell, 1964. Illus. Kazue Mizumura.

Oo Is for Octogon
I Read Signs by Tana Hoban. Greenwillow Books, 1983. Illus. Tana Hoban.
Shapes by Jan Pienkowski. Harvey House, 1975. Illus. Jan Pienkowski.

Pp Is for Patterns
The Amazing Book of Shapes by Lydia Sharman. Dorling Kindersley, 1994.
Hide and Snake by Keith Baker. Harcourt Brace, 1991. Illus. Keith Baker.

Qq Is for Quilt
The Keeping Quilt by Patricia Polacco. Simon and Schuster, 1988. Illus. Patricia Polacco.
The Patchwork Quilt by Valerie Flournoy. Dial Books for Young Readers, 1985. Illus. Jerry Pinkney.
The Quilt Story by Tony Johnston. Putnam, 1985. Illus. Tomie dePaola.

Rr Is for Robot
Get Ready for Robots! by Patricia Lauber. Harper, 1987. Illus. True Kelley.
The Laziest Robot in Zone One by Lillian and Phoebe Hoban. Harper, 1983. Illus. Lillian Hoban.
The Robot Birthday by Eve Bunting. Dutton, 1980. Illus. Marie De John.

Ss Is for Stars
The Falling Stars by Jacob and Wilhelm Grimm. Holt, 1985. Illus. Eugen Sopko.
On a Starry Night by Natalie Kinsey-Warnock. Orchard Books, 1994. Illus. David McPhail.

Tt Is for Teeth
Doctor De Soto by William Steig. Farrar, Straus, & Giroux, 1982. Illus. William Steig.
I Have a Loose Tooth by Sally Noll. Greenwillow Books, 1992. Illus. Sally Noll.
Norman Fools the Tooth Fairy by Carol Carrick. Scholastic, 1992. Illus. Lisa McCue.

Uu Is for Umbrella
The Enchanted Umbrella by Odette Meyers. Harcourt Brace, 1988. Illus. Margot Zemach.
The Umbrella Day by Nancy Evans Cooney. Philomel Books, 1989. Illus. Melissa Bay Mathis.
The Yellow Umbrella by Henrik Drescher. Bradbury Press, 1987. Illus. Henrik Drescher.

Vv Is for Vase
The Magic Vase by Fiona French. Oxford University Press, 1991. Illus. Fiona French.

Ww Is for Watermelon
Leela and the Watermelon by Marilyn Hirsh and Maya Narayan. Crown, 1971. Illus. Marilyn Hirsh.

Xx Is for X-Ray
I Can Be a Doctor by Rebecca Hankin. Children's Press, 1985. Photographs.

Yy Is for Yo-Yo
Alpha Bugs by David Carter. Little, Simon, 1994. Illus. by David Carter.
Yo! Yes? by Christopher Raschka. Orchard, 1993. Illus. Christopher Raschka.

Zz Is for Zebra
Zebra by Caroline Arnold. Morrow, 1987. Photographs by Richard Hewett.
Zebra's Hiccups by David McKee. Simon and Schuster, 1993. Illus. David McKee.